BARRON'S
Junior
Rhyming
Dictionary

First edition for the United States and Canada published
in 2006 by Barron's Educational Series, Inc.

Oxford Junior Rhyming Dictionary
Text copyright © John Foster 2004
Illustrations by Melanie Williamson and Rupert Van Wyk
Copyright © Oxford University Press 2005

This edition of *Oxford Junior Rhyming Dictionary* originally published in the U.K.
in 2005 is published by arrangement with Oxford University Press.

The moral rights of the author have been asserted
Database right Oxford University Press (marker)

All inquires should be addressed to:
Barron's Educational Series, Inc.
250 Wireless Boulevard
Hauppauge, New York 11788
www.barronseduc.com

Library of Congress Control Number: 2005929800

ISBN-13: 978-0-7641-3424-1
ISBN-10: 0-7641-3424-8

Printed in Singapore
9 8 7 6 5 4 3 2 1

Junior
Rhyming
Dictionary

John Foster

Illustrated by
Melanie Williamson
and Rupert Van Wyk

How to use this dictionary

You can use this dictionary to help you find words that rhyme. When you want to find the rhymes for a particular word, the A-Z index on page 146 will help you to find the right page in the dictionary.

You can also use the dictionary to learn how to spell words that belong to the same rhyming family. You will find an index of rhyming sounds on page 143.

The alphabet

The key words in this dictionary are listed in alphabetical order.
There is an alphabet line down the side of each page to help you find your way around the dictionary.

Key words

A key word is a word that you use very often. In this dictionary, the key words are in **bold**. You can look up a key word and find a list of other words that rhyme with it.

Rhyme family

A rhyme family is a family of words that end with the same rhyming sound and have the same spelling pattern.

Each key word belongs to a rhyme family. You will find the rhyming sound after the key word.

Example

key word   *rhyming sound*

hole   *-ole*

rhyme family

mole   pole   role   sole   stole   whole

Sometimes there are several words from one rhyme family that rhyme with words from another rhyme family.

Example

-ole rhymes with *-oal*
coal   foal   goal

-ole also rhymes with *-oll*
poll   roll   scroll   stroll   troll

And sometimes there are words that rhyme with the key word but have a different spelling pattern.

Example

Other words that rhyme with *mole*

bowl   soul

Rhymes

There are lots of rhymes throughout the dictionary. You can use these rhymes as a starting point for rhymes of your own.

A jaguar from Zanzibar
    learned to sing and to play the guitar.
Now he's a famous movie star
    and drives around in a sports car.

Indexes

The dictionary has two indexes. The A-Z index on page 146 lists every word in this dictionary. The key words are printed in **bold** type. This index will tell you the page where you will find the rhyming words you are looking for.

The Index of Rhyming Sounds on page 143 lists every rhyming sound in this dictionary. You can look up the sound that you want to make rhymes with and go straight to the key word in the main part of the book.

Activities

There is an activities section on page 130. These suggest things you can do to practice making up rhymes and writing rhyming poems.

These are the features of the dictionary:

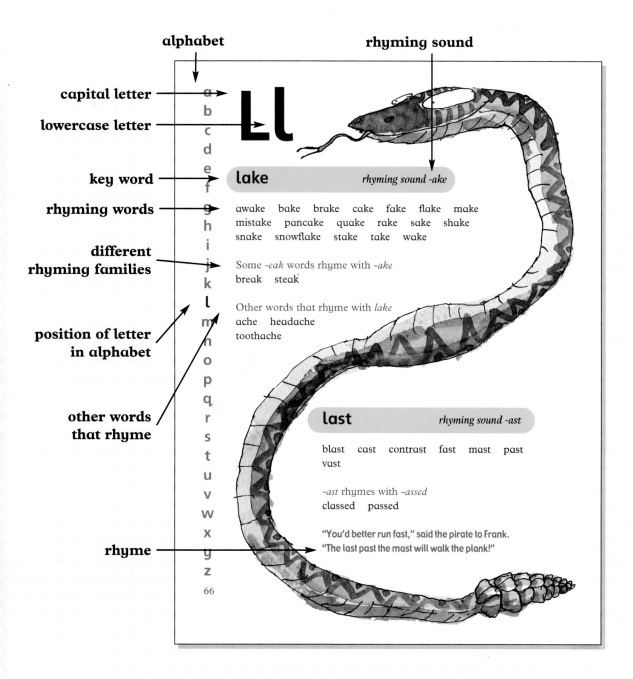

alphabet

rhyming sound

capital letter

lowercase letter

key word

rhyming words

different rhyming families

position of letter in alphabet

other words that rhyme

rhyme

a
b
c
d
e
f
g
h
i
j
k
l
m
n
o
p
q
r
s
t
u
v
w
x
y
z

66

Ll

lake   *rhyming sound -ake*

awake   bake   brake   cake   fake   flake   make
mistake   pancake   quake   rake   sake   shake
snake   snowflake   stake   take   wake

Some *-eak* words rhyme with *-ake*
break   steak

Other words that rhyme with *lake*
ache   headache
toothache

last   *rhyming sound -ast*

blast   cast   contrast   fast   mast   past
vast

-ast rhymes with *-assed*
classed   passed

"You'd better run fast," said the pirate to Frank.
"The last past the mast will walk the plank!"

Aa

act
rhyming sound -act

attract   compact   contact   contract   distract
exact   fact   impact   pact   react   subtract

-act rhymes with *-acked*
backed   backpacked   backtracked   cracked   hijacked
humpbacked   lacked   packed   quacked   sacked   smacked
snacked   stacked   tracked   unpacked   whacked

air
rhyming sound -air

chair   despair   fair   flair   hair   lair   midair   pair
repair   stair   unfair

-air rhymes with *-are*
aware   bare   beware   blare   care   compare   dare   declare
fare   glare   hare   mare   nightmare   prepare   rare   scare
share   snare   software   spare   square   stare

-air rhymes with *-aire*
billionaire   millionaire   solitaire

Other words that rhyme with *air*
bear   pear   prayer   swear   their
there   wear   where

ant
rhyming sound -ant

chant   grant   pant   rant
scant   slant

arm
rhyming sound -arm

alarm   charm   farm   harm

ask
rhyming sound -ask

bask   cask   flask   mask   task

Bb

bang
rhyming sound -ang

boomerang   clang   fang   gang   hang
overhang   pang   rang   sang   slang
sprang   twang

As the midnight bell rang,
the werewolf bared its fang
and **sprang**

bank
rhyming sound -ank

blank   clank   crank   dank   drank
plank   prank   rank   sank   shrank
spank   stank   tank   thank   yank

beach
rhyming sound -each

bleach   each   peach   preach   reach   teach

-each rhymes with *-eech*
beech   screech   speech

My sister gave a loud **screech**
as she bit through the worm in her peach.

belt
rhyming sound -elt

Celt   dwelt   felt   knelt   melt   pelt welt

Another word that rhymes with *belt* is dealt

big
rhyming sound -ig

dig   fig   gig   jig   pig   rig   sprig swig   twig   whirligig   wig

bike
rhyming sound -ike

alike   dislike   hike   like   pike   spike   strike

bird
rhyming sound -ird

gird   third

Other words that rhyme with *bird*
absurd   blurred   heard   herd   nerd   preferred purred   stirred   whirred   word

black

attack   back   backpack   bareback   crack   flapjack
hack   haystack   horseback   jack   knack
lack   lumberjack   pack   piggyback
quack   rack   sack   shack   slack
smack   snack   stack   tack
track   unpack   whack

Other words that rhyme
with *black*
kayak   maniac   plaque
sac   yak

Mr. Black, Mr. Black,
    please can we have our
            ball back?
You can pass it through
            the window.
It'll fit through the crack.
Oh, don't be a spoilsport, Mr. Black.
Please give us our ball back.

bone
rhyming sound -one

alone   clone   cone   drone   lone   megaphone   ozone   phone   postpone   prone   stone   throne   tombstone   tone   trombone   xylophone   zone

-one also rhymes with *-own*
blown   flown   grown   known   own   shown   sown   thrown

Other words which rhyme with *bone*
groan   loan   moan   sewn

"I feel ill," said the king with a groan,
   when he saw the bill for his mobile phone.

boot

rhyming sound -oot

hoot   loot   reboot   root   scoot
shoot   toot

-oot also rhymes with *-ute*
acute   brute   chute   cute   dilute   dispute   execute
flute   mute   parachute   pollute   salute   substitute

Other words that rhyme with *boot*
fruit   newt   suit

An elephant in a parachute.

A koala bear playing the flute.

A penguin whizzing down a chute.

And a hippopotamus in a suit.

boss

rhyming sound -oss

across   albatross   cross   floss   gloss
loss   moss   toss

bounce

rhyming sound -ounce

announce   ounce   pounce   pronounce
trounce

bridge

rhyming sound -idge

fridge   porridge   ridge

Oh, dear! I'm in trouble.
I shouldn't have blown
that bubble gum bubble!

brother

rhyming sound -other

another   mother   other   smother

bubble

rhyming sound -ubble

rubble   stubble

-ubble also rhymes with *-ouble*
double   trouble

Cc

car   *rhyming sound -ar*

afar   ajar   bar   caviar   cigar   far   guitar
jaguar   jar   scar   spar   star   tar

Other words that rhyme with *car*
are   bizarre   mar

A jaguar from Zanzibar
    learned how to play the bass guitar.
Now he's a famous movie star
    and drives around in a racing car!

cart
rhyming sound -art

apart art chart dart depart heart part
smart start tart

catch
rhyming sound -atch

attach batch detach hatch latch match
mismatch patch scratch snatch thatch

cave *rhyming sound -ave*

behave   brave   crave   forgave   gave   grave
knave   microwave   pave   rave   save   shave
slave   wave

"Behave!" said the queen to the naughty knave.
"Or you'll drive me to an early grave!"

coat *rhyming sound -oat*

afloat   boat   float   gloat   goat   moat   oat
throat

-oat rhymes with *-ote*
devote   dote   note   promote
quote   remote   vote   wrote

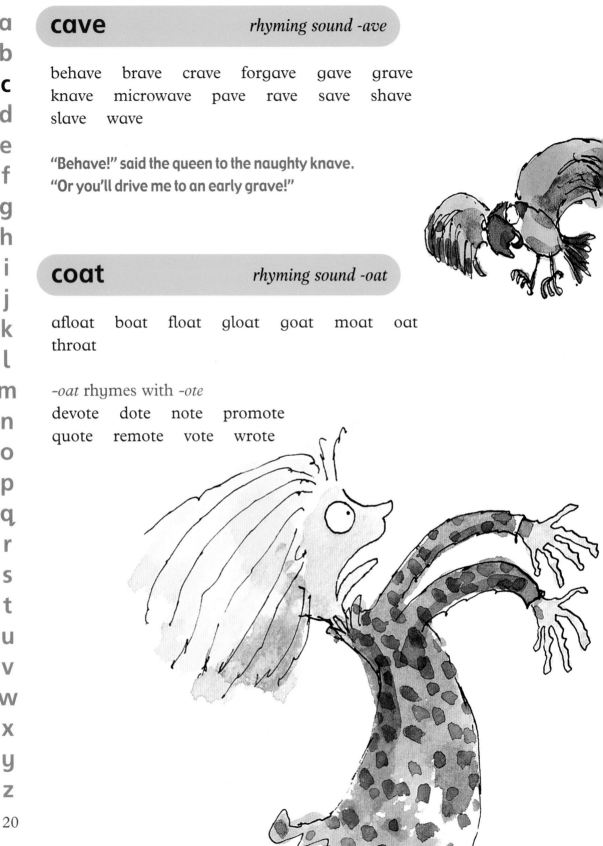

cook

rhyming sound -ook

book brook crook hook look mistook nook rook
shook took

My hands shook
when I saw the evil look
in the eyes of Captain Hook
as he **leaped** from
the page of my book.

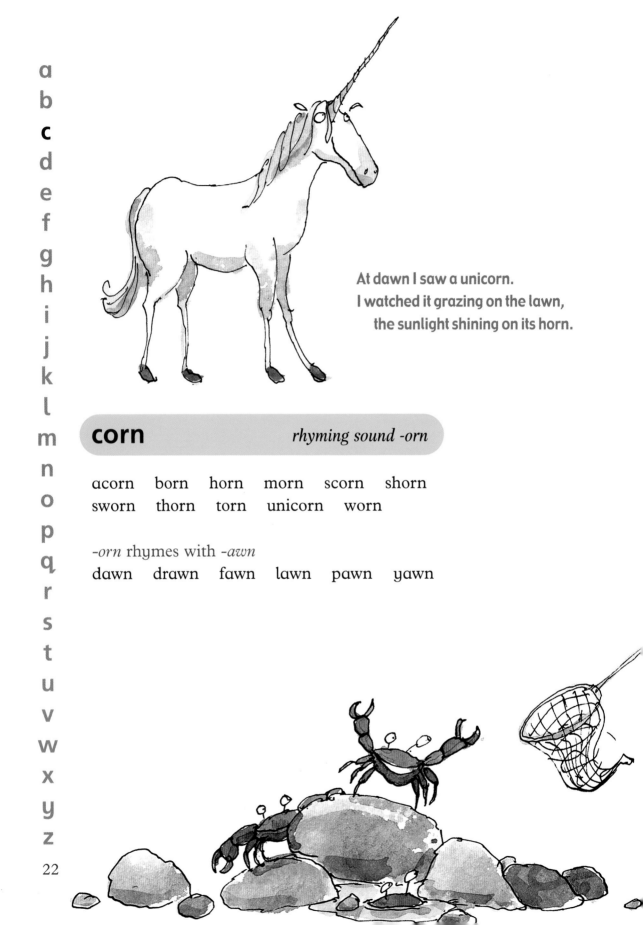

At dawn I saw a unicorn.
I watched it grazing on the lawn,
  the sunlight shining on its horn.

corn   *rhyming sound -orn*

acorn   born   horn   morn   scorn   shorn
sworn   thorn   torn   unicorn   worn

-orn rhymes with *-awn*
dawn   drawn   fawn   lawn   pawn   yawn

cow
rhyming sound -ow

allow bowwow brow eyebrow how meow
now ow! plow vow wow

-ow rhymes with *-ough*
plough

crab
rhyming sound -ab

cab dab drab flab grab jab
lab nab scab slab stab

You mustn't try to grab
  a very bad-tempered crab.
For if you do,
  I'm telling you,
its pincers will give you a jab.

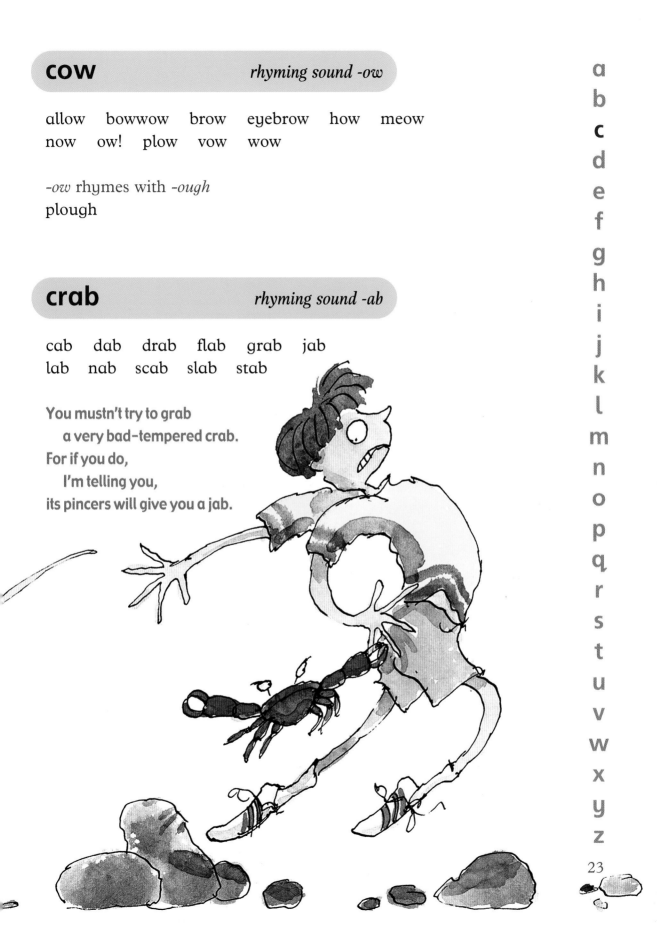

crash

rhyming sound -ash

ash   bash   cash   clash   dash   flash   gash   gnash   hash
lash   mash   rash   sash   slapdash   slash   smash   splash
thrash   trash   whiplash

Lightning flash.

Thunder crash.

Winds lash.

Trees thrash.

Raindrops splash.

Storms smash!

crept   *rhyming sound -ept*

accept   except   inept   intercept   kept   slept
swept   wept

Another word that rhymes with *crept* is
stepped

I slept in, **so I** crept in,
    but Mom saw me, so I was kept in.

Dd

dad
rhyming sound -ad

bad   clad   fad   glad   had   lad   mad
nomad   pad   sad

Another word that rhymes with *dad* is
add

"You're not a bad lad," said dad.
"But your music drives me **mad**!"

dance
rhyming sound -ance

advance   chance   entrance   France   glance   lance
prance   stance   trance

a b c d e f g h i j k l m n o p q r s t u v w x y z

dark

rhyming sound -ark

aardvark ark bark embark hark landmark
lark mark park remark shark spark

"My bite is worse than my bark," said the shark.
"With my teeth I leave my mark!"

dinner
rhyming sound -inner

beginner   inner   sinner   spinner
thinner   winner

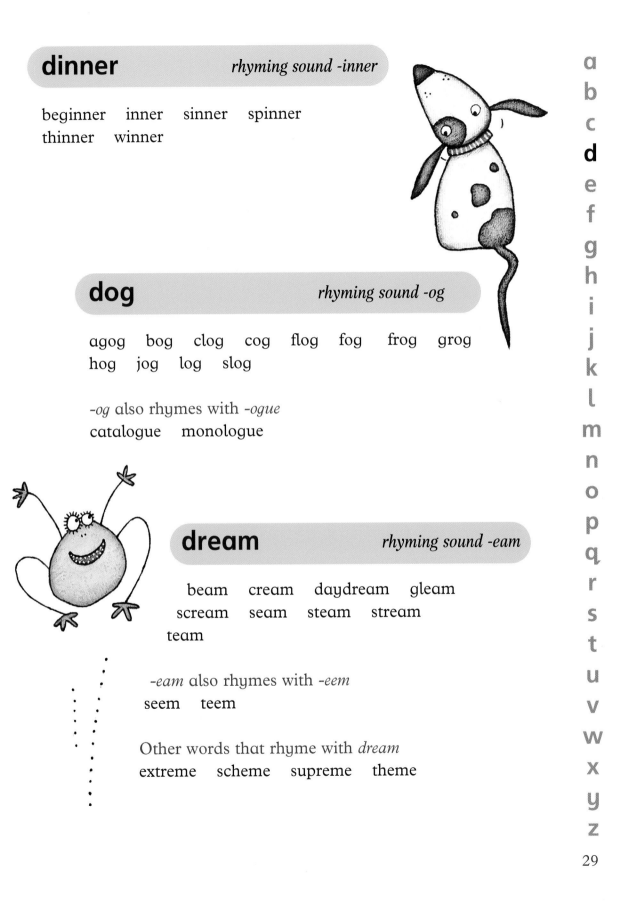

dog
rhyming sound -og

agog   bog   clog   cog   flog   fog   frog   grog
hog   jog   log   slog

-og also rhymes with *-ogue*
catalogue   monologue

dream
rhyming sound -eam

beam   cream   daydream   gleam
scream   seam   steam   stream
team

-eam also rhymes with *-eem*
seem   teem

Other words that rhyme with *dream*
extreme   scheme   supreme   theme

dress   *rhyming sound -ess*

address   bless   chess   confess   depress   distress
excess   express   guess   happiness   helpless   impress
kindness   less   loneliness   mess   oppress   possess
press   princess   progress   stress   success   unless

Another word that rhymes with *dress* is
yes

Nicola Nicholas tore her dress.
Nicola Nicholas couldn't care less.

duck   *rhyming sound -uck*

buck   chuck   cluck   luck   muck   pluck
struck   stuck   suck   truck   tuck   yuck

dust   *rhyming sound -ust*

adjust   bust   crust   disgust
gust   just   must   rust
thrust   trust

Ee

ear   *rhyming sound -ear*

appear   clear   dear   disappear
fear   gear   hear   near   rear
shear   smear   spear

-ear rhymes with *-eer*

beer   buccaneer   career   cheer   deer   engineer   jeer
leer   mountaineer   musketeer   peer   pioneer   sheer
sneer   steer   veer   volunteer

-ear rhymes with *-ere*

atmosphere   here   mere   revere
severe   sincere

Other words that rhyme with *ear*

cashier   cavalier   frontier   pier
souvenir

**We all gave a cheer
   as the wizard made our teacher
disappear.**

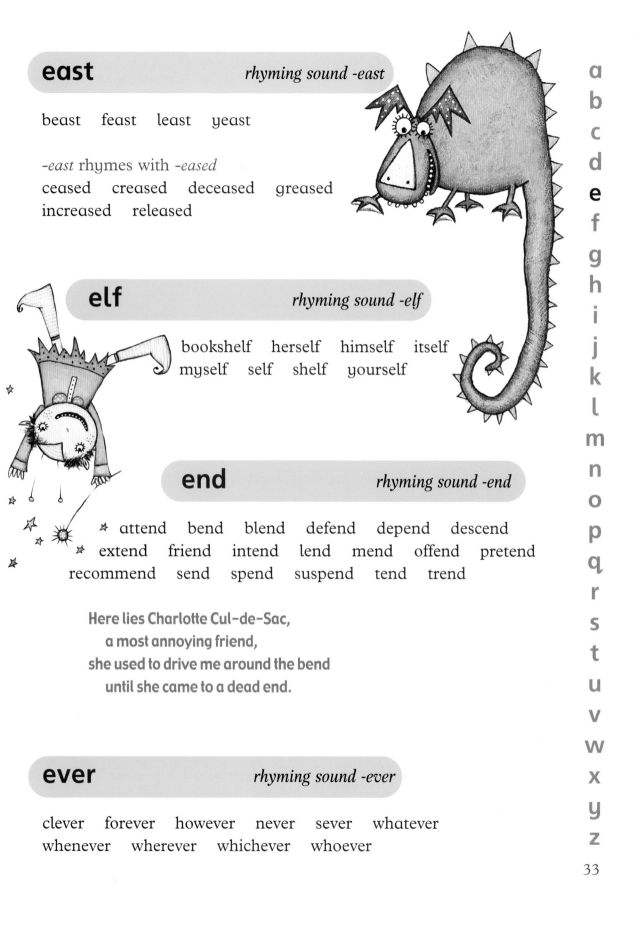

east
rhyming sound -east

beast   feast   least   yeast

-*east* rhymes with -*eased*
ceased   creased   deceased   greased
increased   released

elf
rhyming sound -elf

bookshelf   herself   himself   itself
myself   self   shelf   yourself

end
rhyming sound -end

attend   bend   blend   defend   depend   descend
extend   friend   intend   lend   mend   offend   pretend
recommend   send   spend   suspend   tend   trend

Here lies Charlotte Cul-de-Sac,
   a most annoying friend,
she used to drive me around the bend
   until she came to a dead end.

ever
rhyming sound -ever

clever   forever   however   never   sever   whatever
whenever   wherever   whichever   whoever

Ff

face

rhyming sound -ace

ace brace commonplace disgrace embrace
fireplace grace lace misplace pace place
race replace shoelace space trace

-ace also rhymes with *-ase*
base bookcase case chase database
staircase suitcase

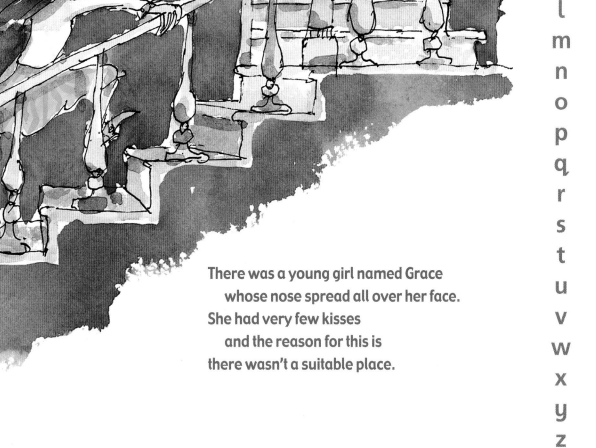

There was a young girl named Grace
   whose nose spread all over her face.
She had very few kisses
   and the reason for this is
there wasn't a suitable place.

find

rhyming sound -ind

behind   bind   blind   grind   kind   mind
remind   rewind   unkind   wind

-ind rhymes with *-ined*
dined   fined   lined   mined   whined

Another word that rhymes with *find* is
signed

When
you stand
in a
line,
it's not
kind
to remind
anyone
you're
behind
that
you're
behind
their
behind.

fire

rhyming sound -ire

admire   bonfire   desire   empire   hire   inspire
spire   squire   tire   umpire   vampire   wire

Other words that rhyme with *fire*
choir   flyer   fryer   higher   liar

Here lies a foolish young squire
who was the most terrible liar.
Caught lying one day
he ran far away
from the heat of his pants on fire!

first
rhyming sound -irst

thirst

Other words that rhyme with *first*
burst   cursed   nursed   rehearsed   worst

fish
rhyming sound -ish

dish   punish   rubbish   selfish
squish   swish   vanish   wish

Three selfish shellfish each had a wish.
The wish each selfish shellfish wished
**   was a selfish shellfish wish.**

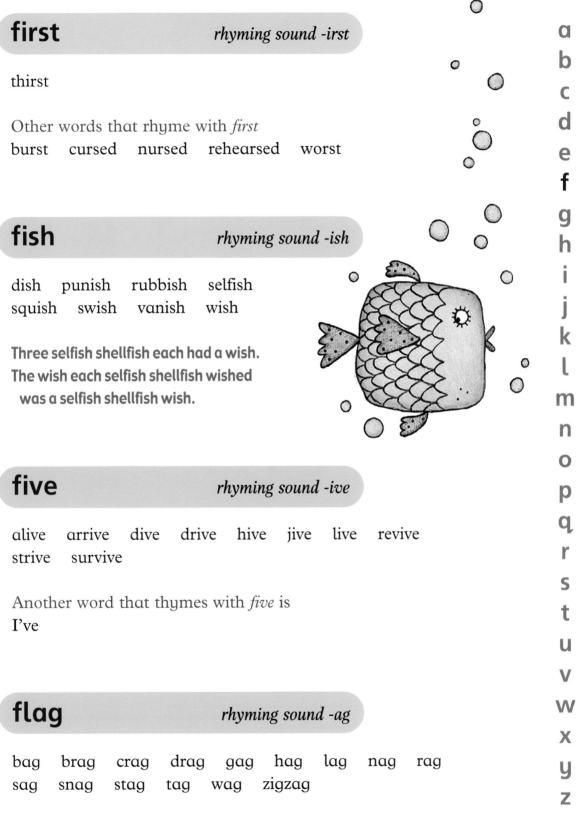

five
rhyming sound -ive

alive   arrive   dive   drive   hive   jive   live   revive
strive   survive

Another word that thymes with *five* is
I've

flag
rhyming sound -ag

bag   brag   crag   drag   gag   hag   lag   nag   rag
sag   snag   stag   tag   wag   zigzag

food   *rhyming sound -ood*

brood   mood

-ood also rhymes with *-ewed*
brewed   chewed   mewed   screwed   viewed

-ood also rhymes with *-ooed*
booed   cooed   mooed   shampooed   shooed
tattooed   wooed

-ood also rhymes with *-ude*
altitude   attitude   crude
exclude   include
intrude   nude   rude
solitude

-ood also rhymes
with *-ued*
argued
barbecued   glued
pursued   rescued
sued

fox

rhyming sound -ox

box   ox   pox

-ox rhymes with *-ocks*

blocks   clocks   docks   flocks   knocks   locks   mocks   rocks
shocks   socks   stocks

Goldilocks wears pretty smocks
   but I wish she'd change her   smelly socks.

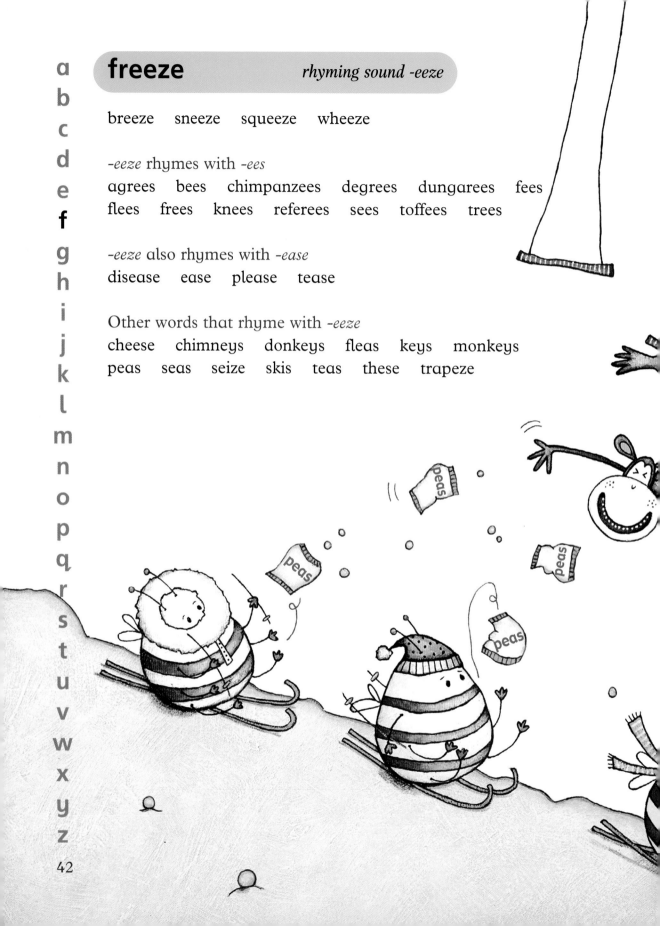

freeze   *rhyming sound -eeze*

breeze   sneeze   squeeze   wheeze

-eeze rhymes with *-ees*
agrees   bees   chimpanzees   degrees   dungarees   fees
flees   frees   knees   referees   sees   toffees   trees

-eeze also rhymes with *-ease*
disease   ease   please   tease

Other words that rhyme with *-eeze*
cheese   chimneys   donkeys   fleas   keys   monkeys
peas   seas   seize   skis   teas   these   trapeze

peas

peas

peas

Chimpanzees in dungarees,
swing with ease on the trapeze,
while bees on skis
struggle to juggle packs of peas.

a
b
c
d
e
f
g
h
i
j
k
l
m
n
o
p
q
r
s
t
u
v
w
x
y
z

fur

rhyming sound -ur

blur   occur   slur   spur

-ur rhymes with *-ir*
fir   sir   stir

-ur also rhymes with *-er*
badger   her   otter
prefer   slipper   tiger

Other words that rhyme with *fur*
purr   were   whirr

Always call a tiger Sir,
    and do not try to stroke his fur,
for tigers are well known to Grrr!

Gg

a
b
c
d
e
f
g
h
i
j
k
l
m
n
o
p
q
r
s
t
u
v
w
x
y
z

gate *rhyming sound -ate*

appreciate   ate   calculate   celebrate   concentrate   confiscate
crate   create   date   debate   decorate   educate   estate
estimate   exaggerate   fascinate   fate   frustrate   grate
hate   investigate   irritate   late   mate   operate   plate
rate   separate   skate   slate   state

-ate also rhymes with *-ait*
bait   wait

Other words that rhyme with *gate*
eight   great   straight   weight

Elephant! Elephant!
Don't try to skate.
The ice is too thin,
   it won't bear your
weight....

Too late!

girl
rhyming sound -irl

swirl   twirl   whirl

-irl rhymes with *-url*
curl   hurl

Other words that rhyme with *girl*
earl   pearl

glass
rhyming sound -ass

brass   bypass   class   grass   pass   trespass

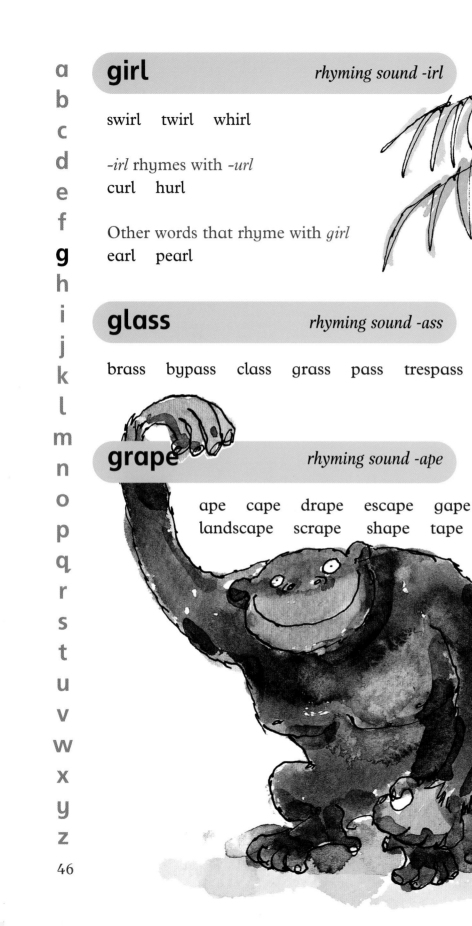

grape
rhyming sound -ape

ape   cape   drape   escape   gape
landscape   scrape   shape   tape

grub

rhyming sound -ub

club   cub   dub   hub   hubbub   pub   rub   scrub   shrub
snub   stub   tub

A grubby grub sat in a tub
   and sang a song
as he had a good scrub.

"I'm a scrub-a-grub, rub-a-dub grub!"

Hh

hairy   *rhyming sound -airy*

airy   dairy   fairy

-airy rhymes with *-ary*
canary   contrary   scary   vary   wary

hand   *rhyming sound -and*

band   brand   expand   gland   grand   land
sand   stand   strand   understand

-and rhymes with *-anned*
banned   canned   fanned   manned   planned
scanned   spanned   tanned

hat

rhyming sound -at

acrobat aristocrat bat brat cat chat combat fat
flat gnat habitat mat pat pit-a-pat rat rat-a-tat
sat spat splat that vat

There was a young fellow named Matt
  who wanted to look like a cat.
His feet were like paws
  with retractable claws
and whiskers grew out of his hat.

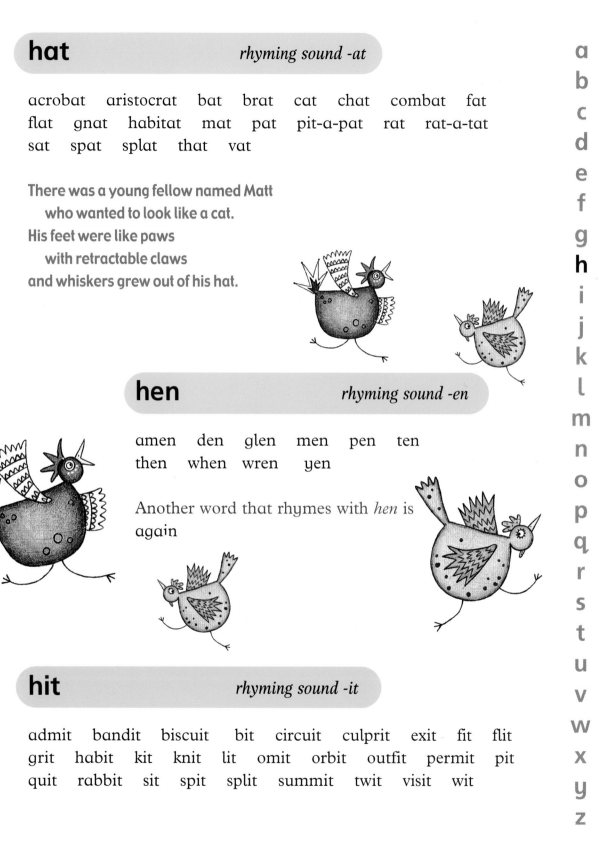

hen

rhyming sound -en

amen den glen men pen ten
then when wren yen

Another word that rhymes with *hen* is
again

hit

rhyming sound -it

admit bandit biscuit bit circuit culprit exit fit flit
grit habit kit knit lit omit orbit outfit permit pit
quit rabbit sit spit split summit twit visit wit

hole

rhyming sound -ole

mole   pole   role   sole
stole   whole

-ole rhymes with *-oal*
coal   foal   goal

-ole also rhymes with *-oll*
poll   roll   scroll   stroll   troll

Other words that rhyme with *hole*
bowl   soul

Old King Cole scored a very fine goal,
    a very fine goal scored he.
A TV poll reckoned King Cole's goal
    was the best you'd ever see.

a b c d e f g h i j k l m n o p q r s t u v w x y z

honey

rhyming sound -oney

money

-oney rhymes with *-unny*
bunny   funny   runny   sunny

I eat my peas with honey.
I've done it all my life.
It makes the peas taste funny,
    but it keeps them on the knife.

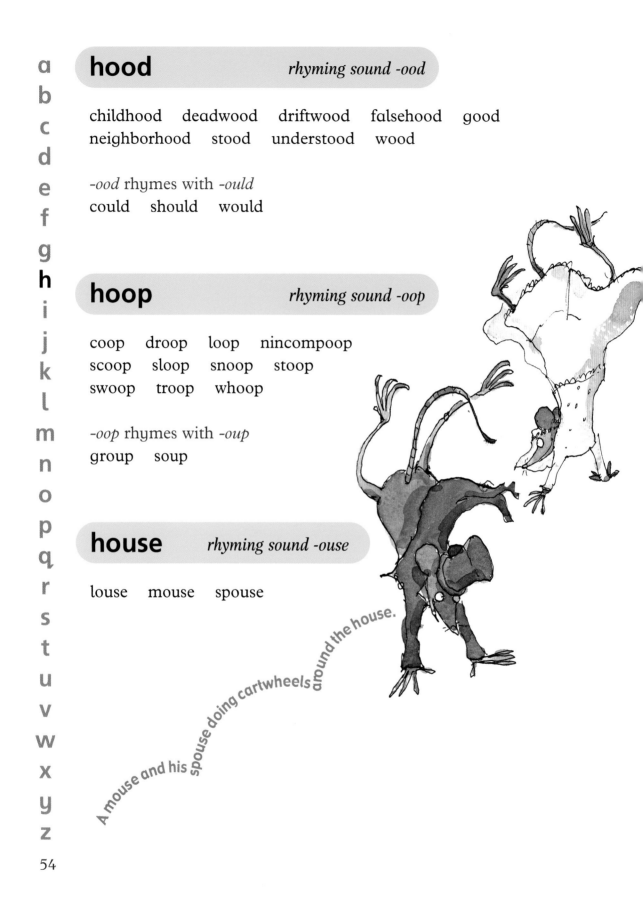

a
b
c
d
e
f
g
h
i
j
k
l
m
n
o
p
q
r
s
t
u
v
w
x
y
z

hood

rhyming sound -ood

childhood   deadwood   driftwood   falsehood   good
neighborhood   stood   understood   wood

-ood rhymes with *-ould*
could   should   would

hoop

rhyming sound -oop

coop   droop   loop   nincompoop
scoop   sloop   snoop   stoop
swoop   troop   whoop

-oop rhymes with *-oup*
group   soup

house

rhyming sound -ouse

louse   mouse   spouse

A mouse and his spouse doing cartwheels around the house.

54

hunt

rhyming sound -unt

blunt   grunt   punt   runt   shunt   stunt

Another word that rhymes with *hunt* is
front

hut

rhyming sound -ut

but   chestnut   cut   doughnut   glut   gut
jut   nut   rut   shut   strut   tut-tut

Another word that rhymes
with *hut* is
putt

a b c d e f g h i j k l m n o p q r s t u v w x y z

55

Ii

ice
rhyming sound -ice

advice   dice   lice   mice   nice   price   rice   sacrifice
slice   spice   splice   twice   vice

The three blind mice said,
   "It's not very nice
of the farmer's wife
   to want to slice
our tails off with her carving knife!"

Other words that
rhyme with *ice*
paradise
precise

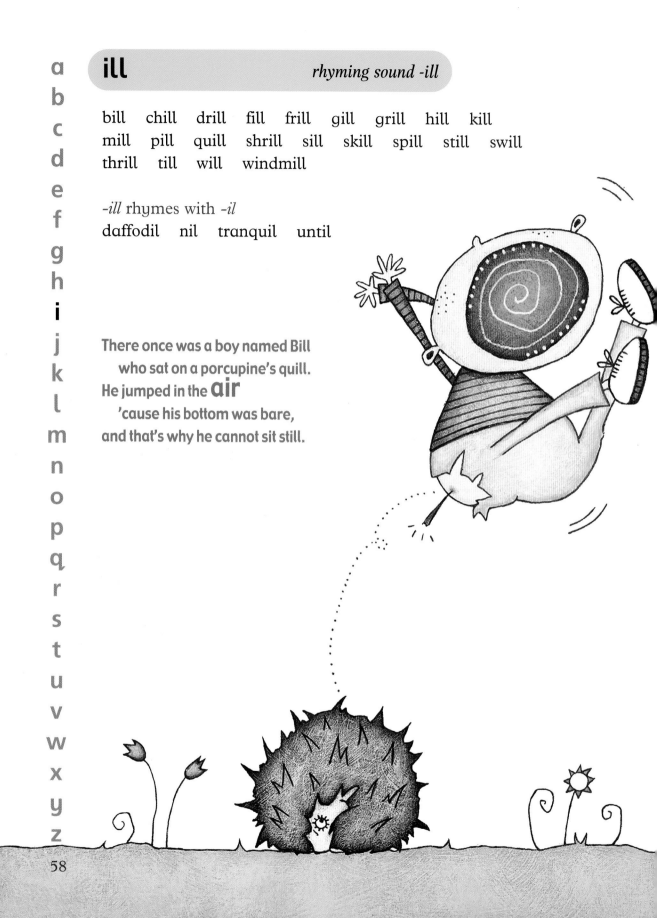

ill

rhyming sound -ill

bill chill drill fill frill gill grill hill kill
mill pill quill shrill sill skill spill still swill
thrill till will windmill

-ill rhymes with *-il*
daffodil nil tranquil until

There once was a boy named Bill
    who sat on a porcupine's quill.
He jumped in the **air**
    'cause his bottom was bare,
and that's why he cannot sit still.

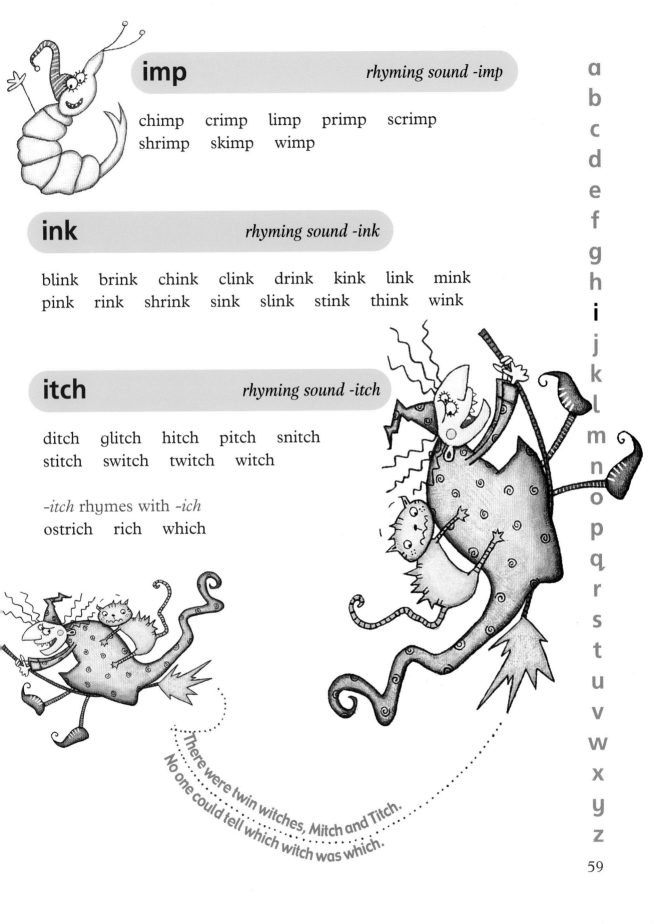

imp

rhyming sound -imp

chimp   crimp   limp   primp   scrimp
shrimp   skimp   wimp

ink

rhyming sound -ink

blink   brink   chink   clink   drink   kink   link   mink
pink   rink   shrink   sink   slink   stink   think   wink

itch

rhyming sound -itch

ditch   glitch   hitch   pitch   snitch
stitch   switch   twitch   witch

-itch rhymes with *-ich*
ostrich   rich   which

There were twin witches, Mitch and Titch.
No one could tell which witch was which.

a b c d e f g h i j k l m n o p q r s t u v w x y z

59

Jj

jam
rhyming sound -am

am cram dam exam gram ham program ram scam scram sham slam swam tram wham yam

Another word that rhymes with *jam* is
lamb

jet
rhyming sound -et

alphabet basket bet bracelet bucket carpet clarinet cricket duet fidget forget fret gadget get helmet Internet jacket let magnet met net pet pocket puppet regret rocket secret set ticket trumpet upset vet wet yet

-et also rhymes with *-eat*
sweat threat

-et also rhymes with *-ette*
baguette cassette launderette omelette

Another word that rhymes with *jet* is
debt

job
rhyming sound -ob

blob   bob   cob   gob   hob   hobnob   knob   lob   mob
rob   snob   sob   throb

jug
rhyming sound -ug

bug   chug   drug   dug   glug   hug   humbug   lug   mug
plug   rug   shrug   slug   smug   snug   thug   tug

A slimy slug drank from a jug.
A grubby bug drank from a mug.
Then the slug gave the *bug* a *hug!*

jump
rhyming sound -ump

bump   clump   dump   hump   lump   plump
pump   rump   slump   stump   thump

Kk

keep

rhyming sound -eep

asleep beep bleep cheep creep deep jeep
peep seep sheep sleep steep sweep weep

-eep rhymes with *-eap*
cheap heap leap reap

I'm a runaway sheep.
I stole the keys to Bo Peep's jeep,
while she was lying fast asleep.
Get out of my way! **Beep! Beep!**

BO PEEP

abcdefghijk**k**lmnopqrstuvwxyz

king

rhyming sound -ing

boring   bring   ceiling   cling   ding   fling   ping   ring
sing   sling   spring   sting   string   swing   thing   wing
wring   zing

When the bee gave the king a sting,
the king did a Highland fling.
So his arm ended up in a sling.

kiss
rhyming sound -iss

amiss   bliss   dismiss   hiss   miss

Other words that rhyme with *kiss*
office   practice   promise   service   this

I'll be good, Mom, just promise me this:
    You won't try to give me a kiss
in the playground. Just give it a miss!

knock
rhyming sound -ock

block   clock   crock   dock   flock   lock   mock
rock   shock   sock   stock   ticktock

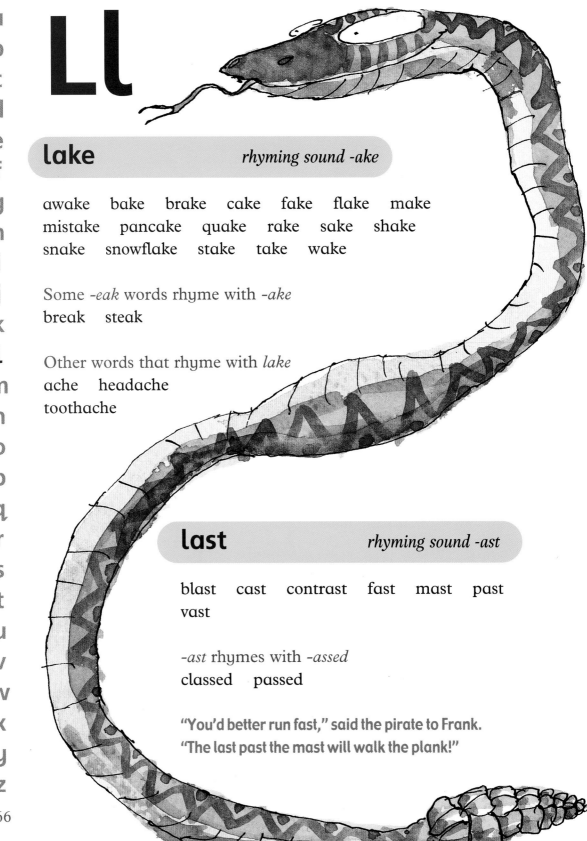

Ll

lake
rhyming sound -ake

awake   bake   brake   cake   fake   flake   make
mistake   pancake   quake   rake   sake   shake
snake   snowflake   stake   take   wake

Some *-eak* words rhyme with *-ake*
break   steak

Other words that rhyme with *lake*
ache   headache
toothache

last
rhyming sound -ast

blast   cast   contrast   fast   mast   past
vast

-ast rhymes with *-assed*
classed   passed

"You'd better run fast," said the pirate to Frank.
"The last past the mast will walk the plank!"

leg

rhyming sound -eg

beg   dreg   keg   nutmeg   peg

Another word that rhymes with *leg* is
egg

lid

rhyming sound -id

bid   did   forbid   grid   hid   liquid   kid   pyramid   rapid
rid   rigid   skid   slid   squid   stupid   timid   undid

I slid back the bolt and undid the locks
to see what lay hid in the secret box.

a
b
c
d
e
f
g
h
i
j
k
l
m
n
o
p
q
r
s
t
u
v
w
x
y
z

67

light

rhyming sound -ight

bright   delight   fight   flight   fright   knight   midnight
might   night   outright   playwright   plight   right   sight
slight   tight   tonight   twilight   upright   uptight

-ight rhymes with *-ite*
appetite   bite   dynamite   excite   ignite   invite
kite   mite   polite   quite   recite   site   spite
unite   white   write

Other words that rhyme with *light*
byte   height

When Dwight Wright had stage fright,
    Mrs. Wright said, "Don't get uptight, Dwight,
it'll be all right on the night."

After the first night, Dwight Wright
    said, "It went all right.
You were quite right, Mrs. Wright."

lord

rhyming sound -ord

afford   chord   cord   ford   record   sword

-ord rhymes with *-oard*
aboard   board   cardboard   hoard   keyboard
scoreboard   skateboard

-ord also rhymes with *-ored*
adored   bored   explored   ignored   scored   snored   stored

Other words that rhyme with *lord*
award   horde   poured   reward   roared   soared   toward
ward

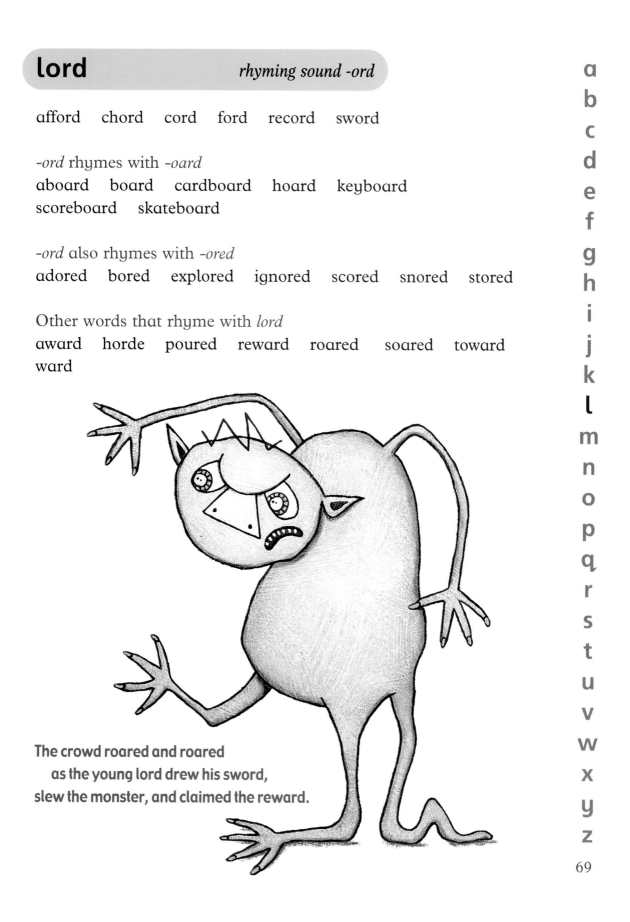

The crowd roared and roared
   as the young lord drew his sword,
slew the monster, and claimed the reward.

love *rhyming sound -ove*

above   dove   glove   shove

lunch *rhyming sound -unch*

brunch   bunch   crunch   hunch   munch   punch   scrunch

lung *rhyming sound -ung*

clung   dung   flung   hung   rung   slung   sprung   strung
stung   sung   swung   wrung

Other words that rhyme with *lung*
among   tongue   young

Mm

map
rhyming sound -ap

cap   chap   clap   flap   gap   kidnap   lap   nap
overlap   rap   sap   scrap   slap   snap   strap   tap
trap   unwrap   wrap   yap   zap

On the Clip Clop Clap,
   all the Flops flip flap,
and the Bongles boogle in the breeze.
The Sniggers snip snap,
   the Trotters trip trap,
and the Somersaults sniff and sneeze.
The Somersaults sniff and sneeze.

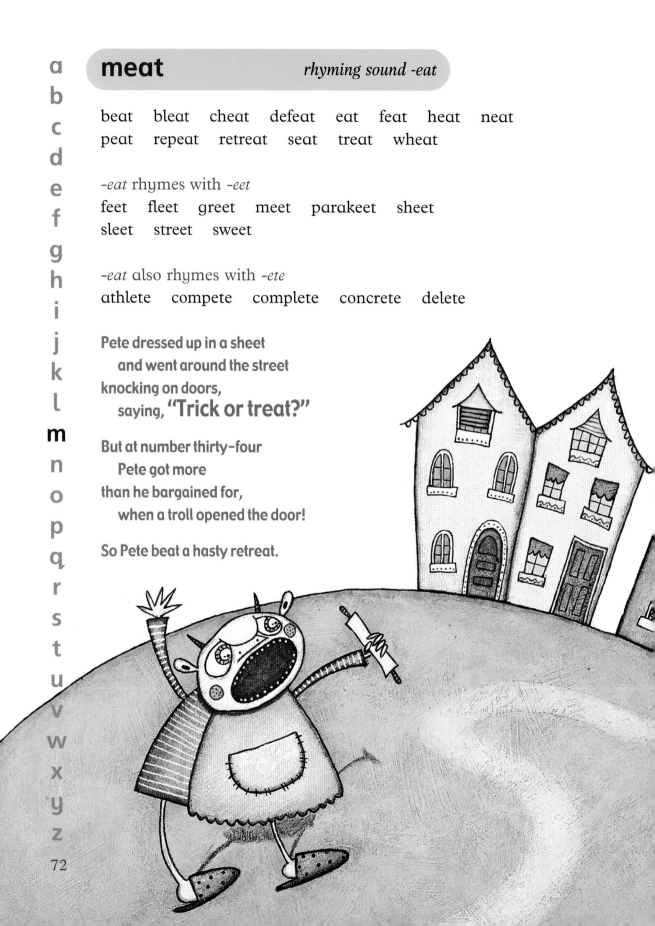

meat   *rhyming sound -eat*

beat   bleat   cheat   defeat   eat   feat   heat   neat
peat   repeat   retreat   seat   treat   wheat

-eat rhymes with *-eet*
feet   fleet   greet   meet   parakeet   sheet
sleet   street   sweet

-eat also rhymes with *-ete*
athlete   compete   complete   concrete   delete

Pete dressed up in a sheet
   and went around the street
knocking on doors,
   saying, **"Trick or treat?"**

But at number thirty-four
   Pete got more
than he bargained for,
   when a troll opened the door!

So Pete beat a hasty retreat.

a
b
c
d
e
f
g
h
i
j
k
l
m
n
o
p
q
r
s
t
u
v
w
x
y
z

merry   *rhyming sound -erry*

berry   cherry   ferry

Other words that rhyme with *merry*
bury   very

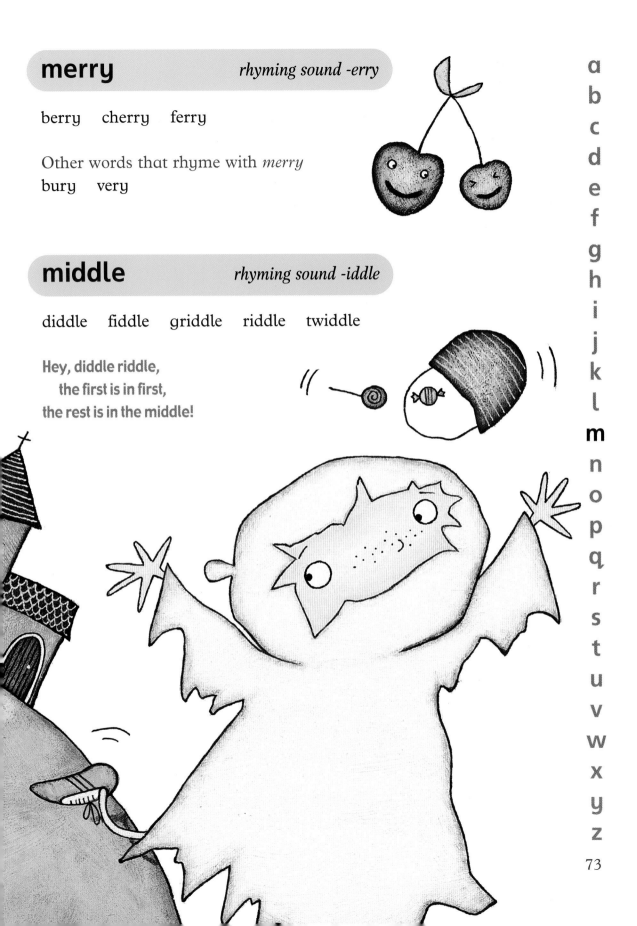

middle   *rhyming sound -iddle*

diddle   fiddle   griddle   riddle   twiddle

Hey, diddle riddle,
  the first is in first,
the rest is in the middle!

a
b
c
d
e
f
g
h
i
j
k
l
m
n
o
p
q
r
s
t
u
v
w
x
y
z

mist   *rhyming sound -ist*

cyclist   fist   insist   list   resist   tourist   twist   wrist

-ist rhymes with *-issed*
dismissed   hissed   kissed   missed

mix   *rhyming sound -ix*

fix   matrix   nix   six

-ix rhymes with *-icks*
bricks   broomsticks   chicks   clicks   flicks   gimmicks
kicks   licks   matchsticks   nicks   picks   pricks   sticks
ticks   tricks

The ghost of the magician said,
    "I'm really in a fix.
The problem is the audience
    sees right through all my tricks."

moon   *rhyming sound -oon*

afternoon   baboon   balloon   bassoon
cartoon   harpoon   honeymoon
lagoon   macaroon   maroon   noon
platoon   raccoon   saloon   soon
spoon   swoon   tycoon   typhoon

A baboon in a saloon
playing a tune on a bassoon.

-oon rhymes with *-une*

dune   fortune   June   Neptune   prune   tune

Another word that rhymes with *moon* is
strewn

mud   *rhyming sound -ud*

bud   cud   dud   spud   stud
thud

Other words that rhyme with
mud
blood   flood

mum   *rhyming sound -um*

chum   drum   glum   gum   hum
plum   rum   slum   strum   sum
swum   tum   yum

-um rhymes with *-umb*
crumb   dumb   numb   plumb   succumb
thumb

Other words that rhyme with *mum*
become   come   some

Nn

name
rhyming sound -ame

became   blame   came   fame   flame   frame   game
lame   same   shame   tame

-ame rhymes with *-aim*
acclaim   aim   claim   exclaim   maim

I am the wizard's dragon.
I speak with tongues of flame.
I am the wizard's dragon.
Firesnorter is my name.

abcdefghijklmnopqrstuvwxyz

3/24/2019

DIAZ LUZ

Item Number: 31901039810876

All Contra Costa County Libraries will be
closed on Sunday, April 21st. Items may
be renewed at ccclib.org or by calling
1-800-984-4636, menu option 1. Book drop
will be open. El Sobrante Library remains
closed for repairs.

Hold Shelf Slip

neck   *rhyming sound -eck*

check   deck   fleck   peck   speck   wreck

Another word that rhymes with *neck* is
trek

"Just let me check," said the vampire.
"I think there's a speck
of blood on your neck."

nettle   *rhyming sound -ettle*

kettle   settle

-ettle rhymes with *-etal*
metal   petal

78

nine

rhyming sound -ine

airline   combine   define   dine   divine   fine   line   mine
pine   recline   shine   shrine   spine   swine   twine   valentine
vine   whine   wine

-ine rhymes with *-ign*
benign   design   resign   sign

It sent a shiver down my spine
   when I received a valentine
saying, "I think you are divine,"

nose   *rhyming sound -ose*

chose   close   expose   hose   pose   prose   propose   rose
suppose   those

-ose rhymes with *-ows*
arrows   bellows   blows   bungalows   crows   elbows
flows   glows   grows   knows   meadows   mows   rows
shadows   shows   slows   snows   stows   throws   tows

-ose also rhymes with *-oes*
dominoes   foes   goes   hoes   oboes   potatoes   tiptoes
toes   tomatoes   volcanoes   woes

-ose also rhymes with *-os*
radios   stereos   videos

Other words that rhyme with *nose*
bulldoze   doze   froze   sews
UFOs

When the winter wind blows,
    an icicle grows on the scarecrow's nose,
and it looks just like Pinocchio's!

Oo

oak

rhyming sound -oak

cloak   croak   soak

-oak rhymes with *-oke*
awoke   broke   choke   joke
poke   provoke   smoke   spoke
stroke   woke   yoke

Other words that rhyme with *oak*
folk   yolk

oil

rhyming sound -oil

boil   broil   coil   foil   recoil   soil   spoil
toil   turmoil

-oil rhymes with *-oyal*
loyal   royal

Another word that rhymes
with *oil* is
gargoyle

old

rhyming sound -old

behold   bold   cold   fold   gold   hold   marigold   mold
scaffold   scold   sold   told

Other words that rhyme with *old*
bowled   consoled   controlled   patrolled   polled   rolled
strolled

"Behold!" said the wizard,
   and he conjured a room full of gold.
But my blood ran cold,
   when he scarily warned,
"My secrets must never be told."

out

rhyming sound -out

about   blackout   bout   clout   dugout   hideout
knockout   lookout   pout   rout   scout   shoot-out
shout   snout   spout   sprout   stout   throughout
trout   without

Other words that rhyme with *out*
doubt   drought

owl

rhyming sound -owl

fowl   growl   howl   prowl   scowl   yowl

-owl rhymes with *-owel*
bowel   towel   trowel   vowel

Another word that rhymes
with *owl* is
foul

Pp

page

rhyming sound -age

age   cage   engage   enrage   outrage   rage
rampage   stage   teenage   upstage   wage

"It's like being on stage.
Let me out or pay me a wage!"
The monkey screeched in a rage
   as it rattled the bars of its cage.

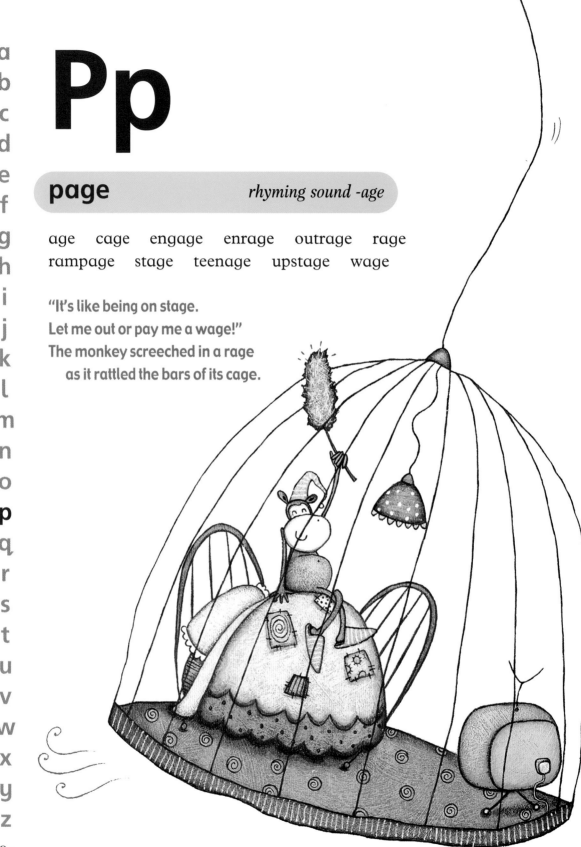

paint
rhyming sound -aint

complaint   faint   saint   taint

paste
rhyming sound -aste

haste   taste   waste

-aste rhymes with *-aced*
braced   chased   disgraced   embraced   faced   graced   laced
paced   placed   raced   replaced   spaced   traced

Another word that rhymes with *paste* is
waist

pond
rhyming sound -ond

beyond   blond   bond   fond   respond

Another word that rhymes with *pond* is
wand

Said the frog in the pond,
   "Please kiss me or wave your wand."
But the princess didn't respond.

pool

rhyming sound -ool

cool   drool   fool   school   spool   stool
tool   whirlpool

-ool rhymes with *-ule*
globule   minuscule   molecule   mule
ridicule   rule   schedule   yule

Other words that rhyme with *pool*
fuel   ghoul

In our school
   there's an empty stool,
where nobody sits
   except the ghoul
of the pupil who died
   while playing the fool.

post

rhyming sound -ost

almost   ghost   host   most
signpost   utmost

-ost rhymes with *-oast*
boast   coast
roast   toast

At the Halloween Ball,
   our host was a ghost
who walked through the wall.

pot
rhyming sound -ot

apricot blot cannot clot cot dot earshot forgot
got hot jackpot jot knot lot mascot not plot
robot rot Scot shot slot snot spot tot trot

Other words that rhyme with *pot*
squat swat what yacht

Ned Nott was shot,
　　and Sam Shott was not.
So it's better to be Shott than Nott.

print
rhyming sound -int

flint footprint glint
hint lint mint
splint sprint
squint tint

puff   *rhyming sound -uff*

bluff   buff   cuff   dandruff   fluff   gruff   handcuff
huff   scruff   scuff   snuff   stuff

Some *-ough* words rhyme with *puff*
enough   rough   tough

pull   *rhyming sound -ull*

bull   full

-ull rhymes with *-ul*
armful   awful   beautiful   careful   cheerful   doubtful
dreadful   faithful   fearful   graceful   harmful   hopeful
joyful   playful   useful   wonderful

Another word that rhymes with *pull* is
wool

Qq

queen
rhyming sound -een

between   canteen   green   screen   seen   sheen   spleen   teen
thirteen   fourteen (etc.)

-een rhymes with *-ean*
bean   clean   glean   lean   mean   wean

-een also rhymes with *-ine*
limousine   magazine   routine   sardine   tangerine   trampoline

-een also rhymes with *-ene*
gene   hygiene   scene   serene

"I'm a queen," said Kathleen.
"We've been filming a scene.
That's my picture in a magazine,
    and over there's my limousine."
"Dream on," said Jean.

quick
rhyming sound -ick

brick   chick   click   flick   gimmick   kick   lick   limerick
pick   prick   sick   slick   stick   thick   tick   trick   wick

-ick rhymes with *-ic*
attic   basic   comic   elastic   electric   fantastic   frantic
garlic   lunatic   magic   music   panic   picnic   plastic   public
supersonic   terrific   tragic

Rr

rain   *rhyming sound -ain*

brain   chain   complain   contain   drain   entertain   explain
gain   grain   main   obtain   pain   plain   refrain   remain
Spain   sprain   stain   strain   train   vain

-ain rhymes with *-ane*
cane   crane   lane   mane   pane   plane   sane   vane

Other words that rhyme with *rain*
rein   vein   reign

**There was a young girl named Elaine
who was dreadfully sick on the train.**

red

bed   bled   bred   fed   fled   led   shed   shred
sled   sped   wed

-ed words rhyme with some *-ead* words
ahead   bread   dead   dread   head   instead
spread   thread   tread   widespread

Another word that rhymes with *red* is
said

"I sped down the hill on my sled,
but I crashed and demolished the shed,"
said Ted, as he lay on the bed
feeling the bump on his head.

a b c d e f g h i j k l m n o p q r s t u v w x y z

91

ride

rhyming sound -ide

aside   astride   beside   bride   collide   countryside   decide
divide   glide   guide   hide   inside   pride   provide   side
slide   stride   tide   wide

-ide rhymes with *-ied*
cried   defied   denied   died   dried   fried   horrified   lied
spied   terrified   tied   tried

Other words that rhyme with *ride*
dyed   eyed   I'd   sighed

river

rhyming sound -iver

deliver   liver   quiver   shiver   sliver

It made me shake.
It made me shiver.
When the robber's ghost

shouted,
"Stand and deliver!"

a b c d e f g h i j k l m n o p q r s t u v w x y z

road

rhyming sound -oad

load   toad

-oad rhymes with *-ode*
code   episode   erode   explode   mode   ode   rode   strode

-oad also rhymes with *-owed*
burrowed   crowed   flowed   glowed   mowed   owed   rowed
showed   slowed   snowed   stowed   towed

Here lies the body of a toad
    who forgot his safety code,
and didn't wait till the traffic slowed
    before he tried to cross the road.

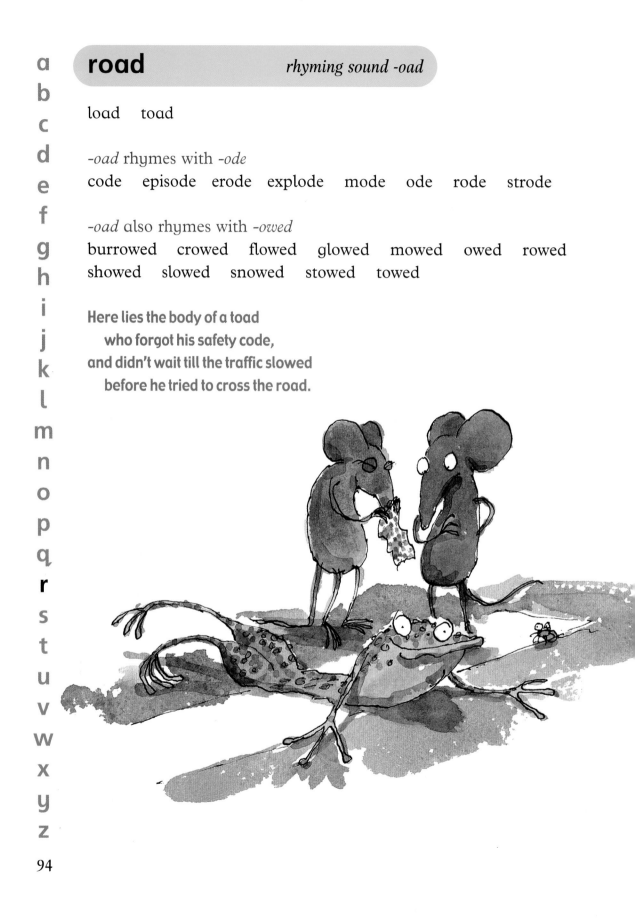

room
rhyming sound -oom

bloom   boom   bridegroom   broom   doom   gloom   groom
heirloom   loom   mushroom   zoom

-oom rhymes with *-ume*
costume   fume   perfume   plume

Other words that rhyme with *room*
tomb   whom   womb

A skeleton once in Khartoum
   invited a ghost to his room.
They spent the whole night
   in the eeriest fight
as to who should be frightened of whom.

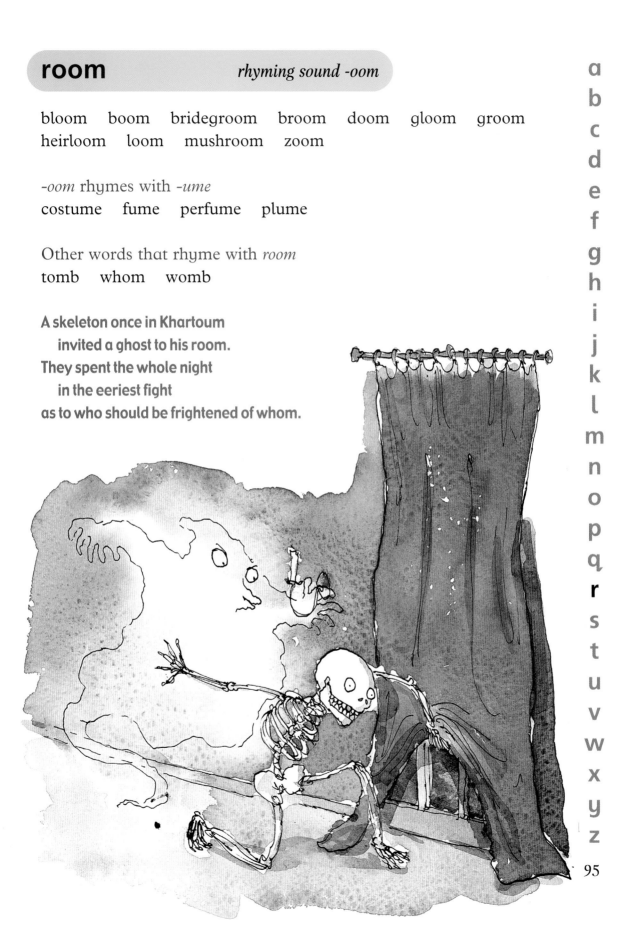

rope   *rhyming sound -ope*

antelope   cope   dope   elope   envelope   grope   hope
horoscope   lope   microscope   mope   pope   scope   slope
telescope   tightrope

Another word that rhymes with *rope* is
soap

" I hope I can cope," said the antelope
     as it started to walk along the tightrope.

round   *rhyming sound -ound*

around   astound   background
bound   found   ground   hound
mound   pound   sound   surround

-ound rhymes with *-owned*
browned   clowned   crowned   downed   drowned
frowned   renowned

My heart begins to pound
     as I spin around and around,
on the whirling, twirling wheel,
     and I wish I was on the ground!

rumble   *rhyming sound -umble*

bumble   crumble   fumble   grumble
humble   jumble   mumble   stumble   tumble

rush

rhyming sound -ush

blush   brush   crush   flush   gush   hush   lush   mush
plush   shush   slush   thrush

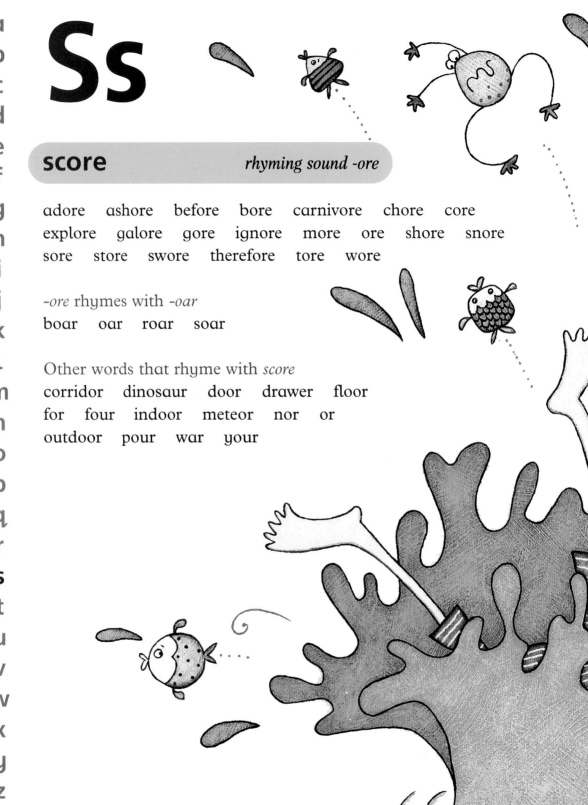

Ss

score
rhyming sound -ore

adore   ashore   before   bore   carnivore   chore   core
explore   galore   gore   ignore   more   ore   shore   snore
sore   store   swore   therefore   tore   wore

-ore rhymes with *-oar*
boar   oar   roar   soar

Other words that rhyme with *score*
corridor   dinosaur   door   drawer   floor
for   four   indoor   meteor   nor   or
outdoor   pour   war   your

shirt

rhyming sound -irt

dirt   flirt   skirt   squirt

-irt rhymes with *-urt*
blurt   hurt   spurt

-irt also rhymes with *-ert*
alert   concert   desert
dessert   expert

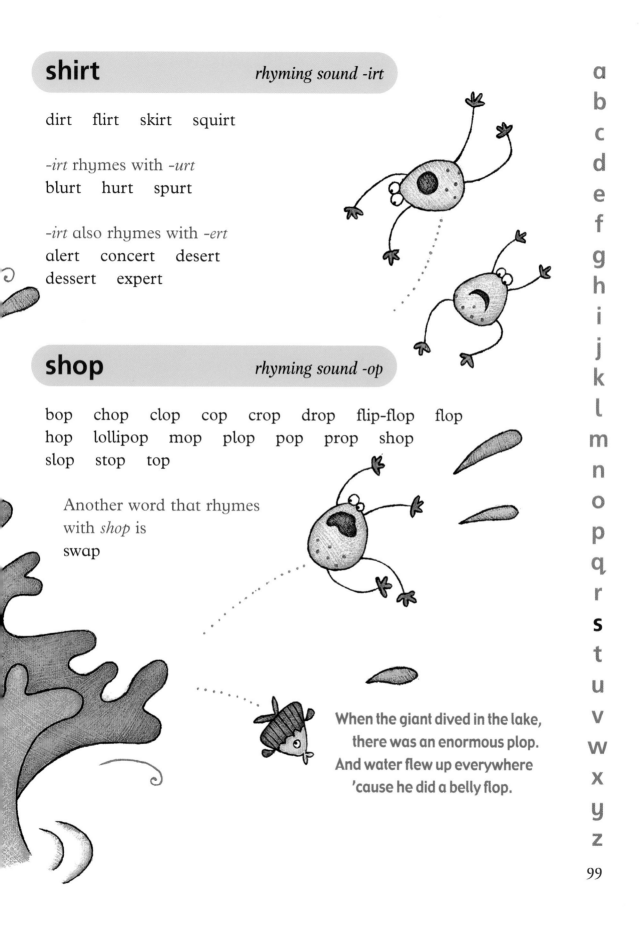

shop

rhyming sound -op

bop   chop   clop   cop   crop   drop   flip-flop   flop
hop   lollipop   mop   plop   pop   prop   shop
slop   stop   top

Another word that rhymes
with *shop* is
swap

When the giant dived in the lake,
there was an enormous plop.
And water flew up everywhere
'cause he did a belly flop.

smile   *rhyming sound -ile*

awhile   crocodile   file
mile   pile   profile
reptile   tile   vile   while

Other words that rhyme with *smile*
aisle   dial   I'll   isle   style   trial

"I'll dine in style," said the crocodile,
    giving a smile,
as he sharpened his teeth with a file.

snow   *rhyming sound -ow*

arrow   below   blow   burrow   crow   elbow   flow
glow   grow   know   low   meadow   mow   pillow
rainbow   row   scarecrow   shadow   shallow   show
slow   sorrow   stow   throw   tomorrow   tow   window

-ow rhymes with *-o*
ago   armadillo   buffalo   commando   disco   domino   echo
go   hello   hero   hippo   logo   macho   mosquito   no   patio
photo   piano   potato   radio   rodeo   so   solo   stereo
studio   tornado   UFO   video   volcano   yo-yo   zero

-ow also rhymes with *-oe*
doe   foe   hoe   mistletoe   oboe   toe   woe

Other words that rhyme with *snow*
although   dough   owe   sew   though

song
rhyming sound -ong

along   belong   long   strong
wrong

spade
rhyming sound -ade

arcade   blade   decade   evade   fade
grade   invade   jade   lemonade   made
marmalade   parade   persuade   shade
trade   wade

-ade rhymes with *-aid*

afraid   aid   braid   laid   maid   mermaid
paid   raid

-ade also rhymes with *-ayed*

arrayed   betrayed   decayed   delayed   frayed   played
prayed   sprayed   stayed   strayed   swayed   x-rayed

Other words that rhyme with *spade*

neighed   obeyed   preyed   suede   surveyed   weighed

Jade shook the bottle of lemonade,
   then she opened it, and we all got sprayed.

a b c d e f g h i j k l m n o p q r **s** t u v w x y z

speak   *rhyming sound -eak*

beak   bleak   creak   freak   leak   peak   sneak
squeak   streak   weak

-eak rhymes with *-eek*
cheek   creek   geek   Greek   leek   meek   peek   reek
seek   sleek   week

-eak also rhymes with *-ique*
antique   boutique   technique   unique

Another word that rhymes with *speak* is
shriek

Two ghosts are playing hide-and-shriek.
They've been seeking each other since last week.

sport

rhyming sound -ort

airport   distort   export   fort   import   passport   port   report
resort   short   snort   sort   support   transport

Sean Short bought some shorts,
   the shorts were shorter than
Sean Short thought.
Sean Short's short shorts were so short
   Sean Short thought, "Sean you ought
not to have bought shorts so short."

Another word that rhymes with *sport* is
court

stamp
rhyming sound -amp

camp   champ   clamp   cramp
damp   lamp   ramp   tramp

storm
rhyming sound -orm

dorm   form   norm   perform   uniform

-orm words rhyme with some *-arm* words
swarm   warm

a b c d e f g h i j k l m n o p q r s t u v w x y z

sun
rhyming sound -un

begun   bun   fun   gun   nun   pun   run   shun   spun   stun

-un words also rhyme with some *-one* words
done   none   one   someone

-un words also rhyme with some *-on* words
son   ton   won

A rabbit raced a turtle.
The turtle easily won.
The rabbit came in second,
a little hot cross bun.

swim
rhyming sound -im

brim   dim   grim   him   rim   skim   slim   trim   whim

Other words that rhyme with *swim*
gym   hymn   limb   synonym

Tt

table   *rhyming sound -able*

able   cable   enable   fable   stable   timetable

Another word that rhymes with *table* is
label

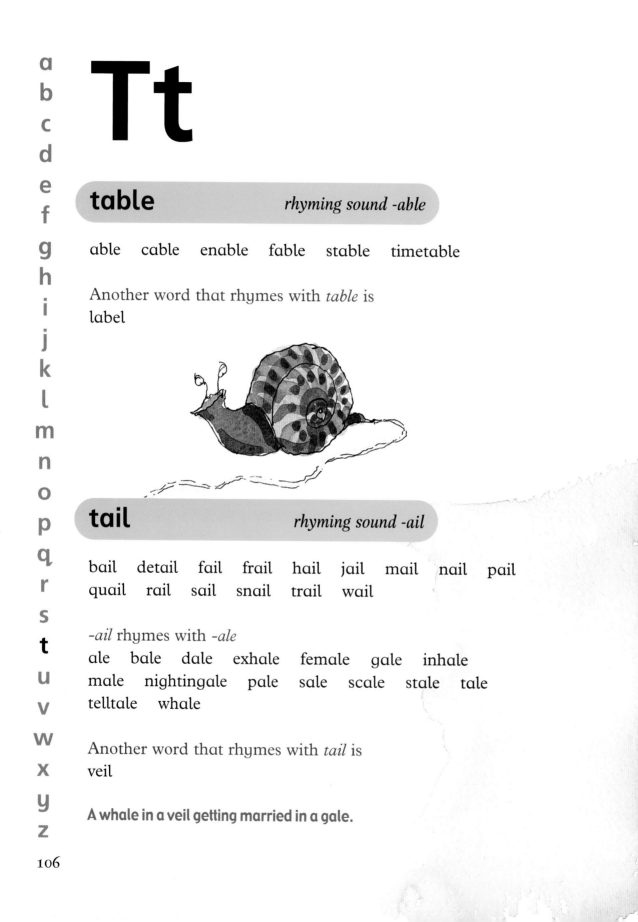

tail   *rhyming sound -ail*

bail   detail   fail   frail   hail   jail   mail   nail   pail
quail   rail   sail   snail   trail   wail

-ail rhymes with *-ale*
ale   bale   dale   exhale   female   gale   inhale
male   nightingale   pale   sale   scale   stale   tale
telltale   whale

Another word that rhymes with *tail* is
veil

A whale in a veil getting married in a gale.

talk

rhyming sound -alk

chalk   stalk   walk

-alk also rhymes with *-awk*
gawk   hawk   squawk   tomahawk

tent

rhyming sound -ent

accident   bent   cement   cent   compliment   consent
content   dent   event   experiment   fragment   frequent
invent   lent   ornament   present   prevent   recent   rent
resent   scent   sent   spent   torment   vent   went

Another word that rhymes with *tent* is
meant

We could not get rid of the scent
    that a cow had left outside the tent!

108

tickle
rhyming sound -ickle

fickle   pickle   prickle   sickle   trickle

Another word that rhymes with *tickle* is
icicle

Don't tickle a thistle or you'll get in a pickle,
   for thistles are prickly and thistles'll prickle.

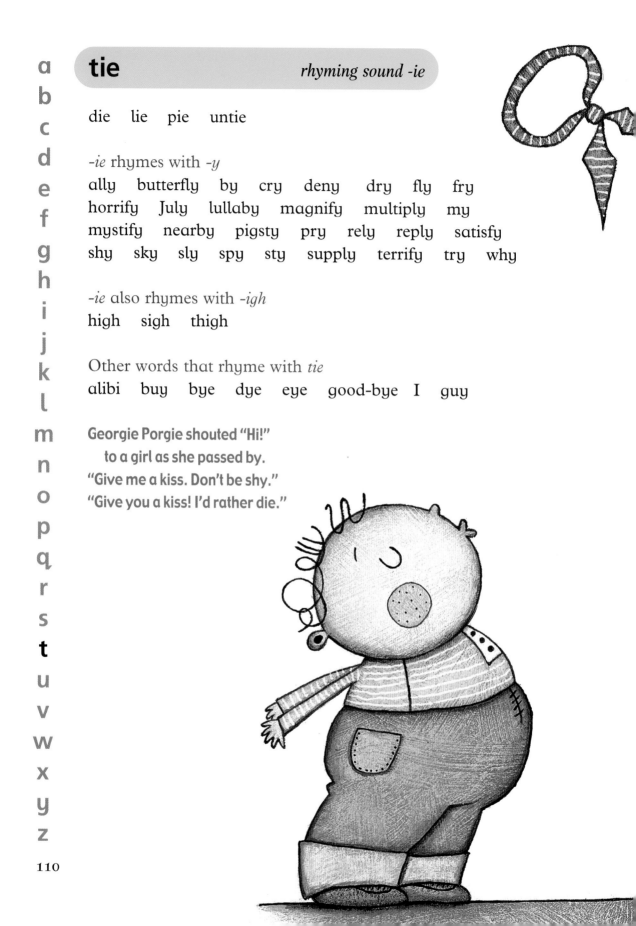

a b c d e f g h i j k l m n o p q r s t u v w x y z

tie
rhyming sound -ie

die   lie   pie   untie

-ie rhymes with *-y*

ally   butterfly   by   cry   deny   dry   fly   fry
horrify   July   lullaby   magnify   multiply   my
mystify   nearby   pigsty   pry   rely   reply   satisfy
shy   sky   sly   spy   sty   supply   terrify   try   why

-ie also rhymes with *-igh*

high   sigh   thigh

Other words that rhyme with *tie*

alibi   buy   bye   dye   eye   good-bye   I   guy

Georgie Porgie shouted "Hi!"
   to a girl as she passed by.
"Give me a kiss. Don't be shy."
"Give you a kiss! I'd rather die."

time
rhyming sound -ime

chime   crime   grime   lime   mime   pantomime
prime   slime

Other words that rhyme with *time*
climb   I'm   rhyme

tower
rhyming sound -ower

cauliflower   cower   flower   power   shower

Some -*our* words rhyme with *tower*
devour   flour   hour   our   scour   sour

a
b
c
d
e
f
g
h
i
j
k
l
m
n
o
p
q
r
s
t
u
v
w
x
y
z

town
rhyming sound -own

brown   clown   crown   down   drown   frown   gown

Another word that rhymes with *town* is
noun

toy
rhyming sound -oy

ahoy   annoy   boy   convoy   corduroy
cowboy   destroy   employ   enjoy   joy   ploy

tree
rhyming sound -ee

agree   bee   chimpanzee   coffee   degree   disagree
fee   flee   free   glee   guarantee   jamboree   jubilee
knee   pedigree   referee   refugee   see   spree
tee   three   toffee   wee

-ee rhymes with *-ea*
flea   pea   plea   sea   tea

Other words that rhyme with *tree*
be   chimney   donkey   genie   graffiti
he   honey   key   macaroni   me   money
monkey   pixie   recipe   she   ski
valley   we

trunk

rhyming sound -unk

bunk   chipmunk   chunk   clunk   drunk   dunk   hunk   junk
punk   shrunk   skunk   slunk   stunk   sunk

Another word that rhymes with *trunk* is
monk

"After the skunk slunk over my bunk,
   it stunk!" said the monk.

Uu

a b c d e f g h i j k l m n o p q r s t u v w x y z

under
rhyming sound -under

blunder   plunder   thunder

Another word that rhymes with *under* is
wonder

The pirates made a dreadful blunder
   by trying to hide all their plunder
beneath a tree during the thunder.
Now they're lying six feet under!

up
rhyming sound -up

buttercup   cup   hiccup   pickup   pup

loot

114

urn

rhyming sound -urn

burn   churn   return   spurn   turn

-urn rhymes with *-earn*
earn   learn   yearn

-urn also rhymes with *-ern*
concern   fern   stern

us

rhyming sound -us

bonus   bus   cactus   circus   genius   hippopotamus
minus   octopus   plus   pus   radius   thus   virus   walrus

-us rhymes with *-uss*
discuss   fuss

-us also rhymes with *-ous*
anxious   courageous   curious   enormous   fabulous
famous   furious   glorious   gorgeous   hideous   hilarious
horrendous   jealous   marvelous   mischievous   monstrous
mysterious   nervous   obvious   precious   serious
tremendous   various

**The driver caused an awful fuss
   when we tried to board the bus
with our hippopotamus.**

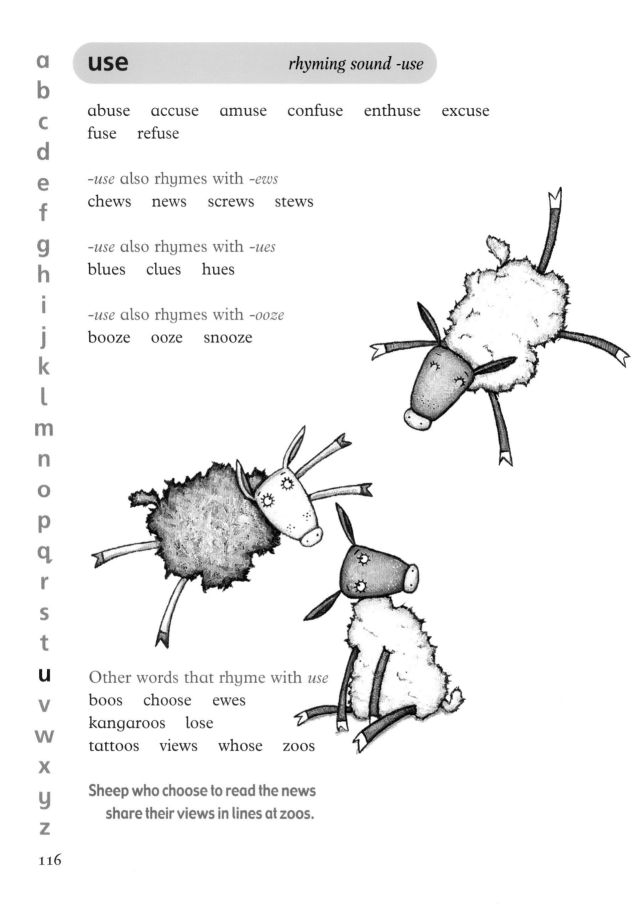

use

rhyming sound -use

abuse   accuse   amuse   confuse   enthuse   excuse
fuse   refuse

-use also rhymes with *-ews*
chews   news   screws   stews

-use also rhymes with *-ues*
blues   clues   hues

-use also rhymes with *-ooze*
booze   ooze   snooze

Other words that rhyme with *use*
boos   choose   ewes
kangaroos   lose
tattoos   views   whose   zoos

**Sheep who choose to read the news
share their views in lines at zoos.**

Vv

van
rhyming sound -an

an   ban   began   bran   can   caravan   clan   deadpan
fan   Japan   man   marzipan   orangutan   pan   plan
ran   scan   span   tan   than

A young man who came from Japan,
   taught his orangutan to cancan.
When I asked if he can,
   the young man from Japan
Said, "Can he cancan? Yes, he can!"

vest

rhyming sound -est

arrest best chest conquest contest detest
digest guest infest invest jest lest nest
pest protest quest request rest suggest
test west zest

-est rhymes with *-essed*

addressed blessed confessed
depressed distressed dressed
expressed guessed impressed
messed obsessed
possessed pressed
progressed
stressed

Ww

wall · *rhyming sound -all*

all   ball   call   fall   football   hall   mall   small
squall   stall   tall

-all rhymes with *-awl*
bawl   brawl   crawl
drawl   scrawl   shawl
sprawl

-all also rhymes with *-aul*
caterwaul   haul   maul

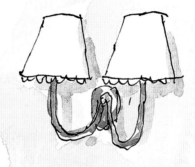

There was a young fellow named Paul,
  who went to a fancy dress ball.
But he made a mistake
  'cause he went as a cake,
and a dog ate him up in the hall.

weed

rhyming sound -eed

agreed   bleed   breed   creed   deed   exceed
freed   greed   guaranteed   heed   indeed   need
reed   refereed   seed   speed   steed   succeed   tweed

-eed words rhyme with some *-ead* words
bead   knead   plead

-eed words rhyme with some *-ede* words
centipede   concede   millipede   stampede   Swede

well

rhyming sound -ell

bell   cell   dwell   farewell   fell   hell   sell
shell   smell   spell   swell   tell   unwell   yell

Other words that rhyme with *well*
caramel   carousel   excel   gel   hotel
lapel   motel   parallel
propel   rebel

Spinning around on the carousel,
sound the horn and ring the bell.
Feel the fairground's magic spell,
spinning around on the carousel.

wheel   *rhyming sound -eel*

feel   heel   keel   kneel   peel   reel   steel

-eel rhymes with *-eal*
appeal   conceal   deal   heal   ideal   meal   ordeal
peal   real   reveal   seal   squeal   steal   veal

win   *rhyming sound -in*

begin   bin   cabin   chin   coffin   din   dolphin   fin   goblin
gremlin   grin   javelin   kin   margin   muffin   origin   penguin
pin   puffin   pumpkin   robin   ruin   satin   sequin   shin   sin
skin   spin   thin   tin   twin   violin
vitamin   within

Other words that rhyme with *win*
examine   inn

**When Violet plays her violin,
  she makes a really awful din.
I'm glad she hasn't got a twin!**

wise

rhyming sound -ise

advertise   advise   arise   clockwise   disguise
exercise   likewise   revise   rise   sunrise   surprise

-ise rhymes with *-ies*
cries   dies   dries   flies   fries   horrifies   lies   lullabies
petrifies   pies   replies   skies   spies   terrifies   ties   tries

-ise also rhymes with *-ize*
apologize   capsize   hypnotize   idolize
organize   prize   realize   recognize   size

Other words that rhyme with *wise*
buys   eyes   highs   sighs   thighs

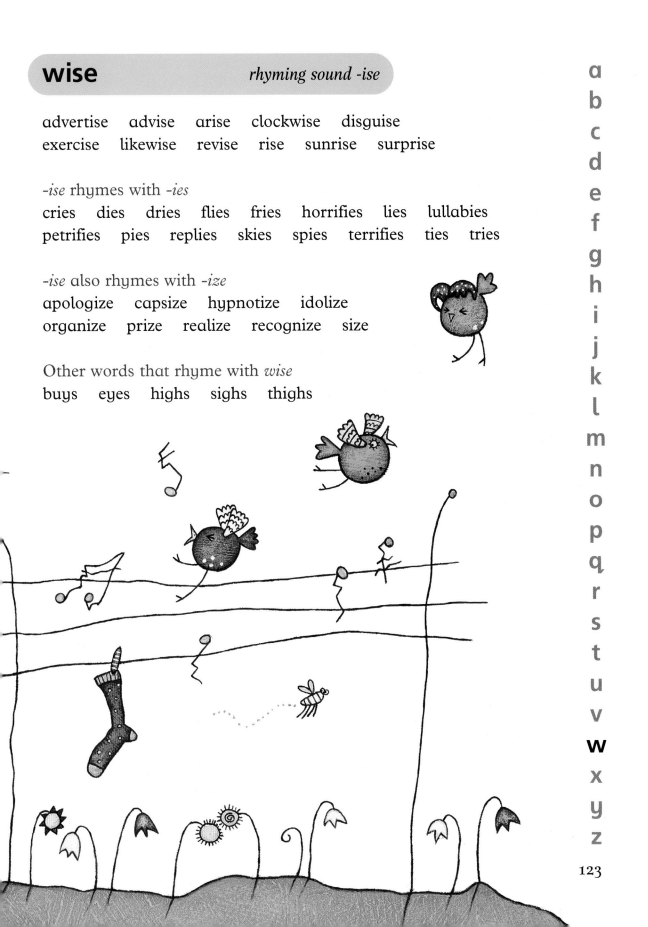

Xx

X ray

rhyming sound -ay

alleyway   anyway   away   bay   betray   birthday
clay   day   decay   delay   display   essay   fray
gray   hay   highway   holiday   hooray
hurray   lay   may   midday   Monday (etc.)
okay   pay   pray   railway   ray   say
spray   stay   stowaway   straightaway
subway   sway   takeaway   today
tray   way   yesterday

-ay rhymes with *-eigh*
neigh   sleigh   weigh

-ay also rhymes with *-ey*
disobey   hey   obey
prey   survey   they

Other words that rhyme with *X ray*
ballet   bouquet   buffet
café   chalet   croquet
fiancé(e)   pâté
ricochet

When Auntie Fay began to neigh
and spend the day just eating hay,
my uncle said, "I cannot say
why she's behaving in this way.
I'd better put her in the stable
in the stall next to your Auntie Mabel."

a
b
c
d
e
f
g
h
i
j
k
l
m
n
o
p
q
r
s
t
u
v
w
x
y
z

Yy

yard   *rhyming sound -ard*

bombard   card   discard   hard
lard   leotard   postcard   regard

-ard rhymes with *-arred*
barred   charred   jarred   marred
scarred   sparred   starred   tarred

Another word that rhymes with *yard* is
guard

yellow   *rhyming sound -ellow*

bellow   fellow   mellow

Other words that rhyme with *yellow*
cello   hello

I was practicing playing the cello,
   when I heard someone give a loud bellow,
"For goodness sake,
   you make my ears ache.
Please stop it. There's a good fellow!"

Zz

zip
rhyming sound -ip

blip   championship   chip   clip   dip   drip   equip   fingertip
flip   friendship   gossip   grip   hardship   hip   kip   leadership
lip   microchip   nip   rip   ship   sip   skip   slip   snip   strip
tip   trip   tulip   whip

zoo
rhyming sound -oo

bamboo   boo   coo   cuckoo   hullaballoo   igloo   kangaroo
moo   shampoo   shoo   tattoo   too   voodoo   woo   yoo-hoo

-oo rhymes with *-ew*
blew   brew   chew   corkscrew   crew   dew   drew   few
flew   grew   interview   knew   mew   nephew   new   pew
phew   screw   shrew   slew   threw   view

-oo also rhymes with *-ue*
argue   avenue   barbecue   blue   clue   continue   cue
due   flue   fondue   glue   hue   revue   statue   subdue
sue   tissue   true   value   venue

Other words that rhyme with *zoo*
canoe   do   ewe   flu   guru
Hindu   menu   Peru
rendezvous   shoe
through   to   tutu
two   you

There was an old man from Peru
    who dreamed he was eating his shoe.
He woke in the night
    in a terrible fright
and found it was perfectly true.

a b c d e f g h i j k l m n o p q r s t u v w x y z

Write your own poetry

Limericks

A limerick is a five-line verse that follows a set pattern. It was
first made famous by the poet Edward Lear (1812-1888). You can
find an example of a limerick on page 129 (**There was an old man
from Peru**).

In a limerick
- ▸ lines 1 and 2 are longer lines that end with a rhyme
- ▸ lines 3 and 4 are shorter lines that end with a rhyme
- ▸ line 5 is a longer line that rhymes with lines 1 and 2

Can you complete these limericks?

> **There was a young schoolboy named Flynn**
> **who sat on a drawing pin.**
> **He leaped up in the air ...**

You can find words with the rhyming sound -*in* listed under the entry
for **win** on page 122 and words with the rhyming sound -*air* under
the entry for **air** on page 8.

> **A daring young girl from Dundee ...**

You can find words with the rhyming sound -*ee* listed under the entry
for **tree** on page 112.

> **A wizard's apprentice named Matt ...**

You can find words with the rhyming sound -*at* listed under the entry
for **hat** on page 49.

Now see if you can make up a limerick on your own. Try to think of a
funny punch line to end it.

Nonsense nursery rhymes

Nonsense nursery rhymes are modern versions of traditional nursery rhymes. For example:

Mary had a little cow.
She fed it safety pins,
    and every time she milked the cow,
the milk came out in tins.

Here are the first lines of some nonsense nursery rhymes.
Can you complete them?

▸ Mary had a little cat.
   She dressed it in a skirt ...

▸ Little Miss Kettle
      sat on a nettle ...

▸ Humpty Dumpty sat on the sofa
      watching cartoons on TV ...

▸ Billy, my brother, and I fell out
   and what do you think it was all about?

▸ Little Tom Tarpet sat on the carpet
      licking a big ice cream ...

▸ Dr. Lester went to Chester ...

▸ Little Bo Peep can't get to sleep ...

▸ Monday's child has a goofy grin ...

Counting rhymes

A counting rhyme is a rhyme that includes counting.
Some rhymes count up to ten, others count backward from ten
down to one.

Can you complete these counting rhymes?

One, two

> One, two,
>   a bath full of glue.
>
> Three, four ...

Ten Naughty Dragons

> Ten naughty dragons blowing smoke rings in a line,
>   one set himself on fire, then there were nine.
>
> Nine naughty dragons ...

Animal Counting Rhyme

> One for the goat in a winter coat.
> Two for the ants in striped underpants ...
> Three for the ...

Ten Young Children

> Ten young children
>   playing in the park.
> The first one said,
>   "Pretend I'm a shark."
> The second one said,
>   "I'm a dinosaur."
> The third one said ...

Rhyming riddles

The poems on this page are rhyming riddles. Can you solve them?

1

I can spin. I can roll. I can fly through the air.
I go where you hit me. Then I lie waiting there.
I am usually round—sometimes big, sometimes small.
I can make my way over or back from a wall.

2

My first is in ghoul and also in charm.
My second is in magic and twice in alarm.
My third is in cauldron but isn't in fire.
My fourth is in gremlin but not in vampire.
My fifth is in skeleton and in bones.
My sixth is in werewolf but isn't in groans.
My seventh is in spell but not in broomstick.
My eighth's found in treat, but not found in trick.
My ninth is in phantom but isn't in fear.
My whole is the scariest night of the year.

3

Hold it steady in your hand,
    then you will see another land,
where right is left, and left is right,
    and no sound stirs by day or night;
when you look in, yourself you'll see,
    yet in that place you cannot be.

Here is a riddle about an animal with the rhyming words missing. Can you work out what the words are and what the animal is?

> I scratch the leaves that have fallen ____
> I am hard to see as my spines are ____
> I use the strong claws upon my ___
> To search for insects and slugs to ___
> Soon I'll curl in a ball in my ____
> And go to sleep for my winter ____

Make up a rhyming riddle of your own. Either choose a subject yourself or write a riddle about an animal or an object, such as a pen, a book, or a bicycle.

Epitaphs

An epitaph is a verse written about a person or animal who has died. It is often put on their gravestone. Here are some examples:

> Here lies the body
>   of Percy Thistle,
> a ref who's blown
>   his final whistle.

> Here lies a teacher, Mr. Lee,
>   who said, "You'll be the death of me!"
> And sitting at his desk one day,
>   he gave a sigh and passed away.

> In loving memory of Rover,
>   who ran out in the road
> and got run over.

Answers: down brown feet eat nest rest a hedgehog

In memory of Charlotte Cul-de-sac,
a loyal and trusted friend,
who finally lived up to her name
and came to a dead end.

Can you complete these epitaphs?

▸ Here lie the remains of Auntie Vi,
who strapped on wings and tried to fly ...

▸ In memory of Billy Green,
who took off in a time machine ...

▸ Here lies what's left of Mr. Bloor ...

▸ Here lies a careless boy named Jake ...

▸ In memory of fearless Fred ...

▸ In memory of Little Red Riding Hood ...

Can you write some epitaphs of your own?

You could write about a person or an animal—either
real or imaginary. For example, you could write about a
nursery rhyme character, such as Old King Cole, an
imaginary creature, such as Desmond Dinosaur, or a
person with an unusual name, such as Candy Bar.

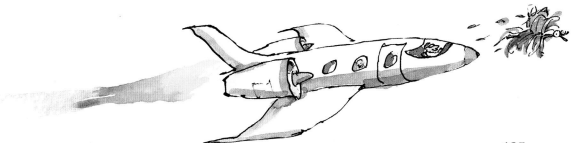

Rapping

Rapping is a popular type of rhyming poetry. A rap is a poem with plenty of rhyming and a very strong rhythm, which is often written to be performed.

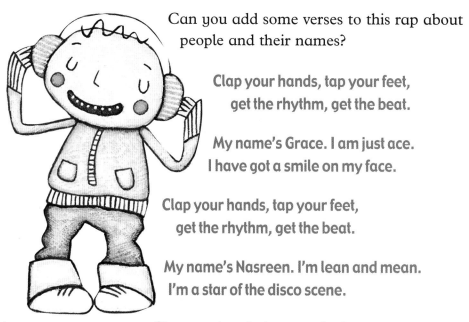

Can you add some verses to this rap about people and their names?

Clap your hands, tap your feet,
   get the rhythm, get the beat.

My name's Grace. I am just ace.
I have got a smile on my face.

Clap your hands, tap your feet,
   get the rhythm, get the beat.

My name's Nasreen. I'm lean and mean.
I'm a star of the disco scene.

Clap your hands, tap your feet,
get the rhythm, get the beat ...

Can you write a fairground rap?
Here are two lines that you can use to get started:

C'mon everybody, let's go to the fair,
   there's plenty of things for us to do there ...

You can write a rap about any topic.
Choose your own subject and write a rap about it.
You could use these two lines to start your rap:

Come on everybody, let's hear you clap,
   we're going to do the ... rap.

Rhyming couplets

One of the ways poets use rhymes is to write rhyming couplets.
A rhyming couplet is a pair of lines that rhyme.

Example:
> We like riding on the double-decker bus,
>> up on the top deck, that's the place for us!

Can you add some rhyming couplets to this list poem?

In my magic box

> In my magic box, I will put

> The twang of a guitar,
>> the silver lining of a star.

> The juicy ripeness of a peach,
>> the sunlight shining on a beach …

Here is cautionary rhyme, written in couplets:

Warning: Too Much TV Can Damage Your Health

> This is the tale of Millie Mee,
>> who day and night would watch TV.
> Now both her eyeballs have turned square,
>> an aerial's growing in her hair.
> All she can do is watch TV,
>> for Millie's glued to the settee.
> So switch off now. Don't hesitate.
> Make sure you don't share Millie's fate.

Can you write some more couplets to complete these cautionary
rhymes?

This is the tale of Samuel Sprocket,
who set off in his homemade rocket ...

This is the tale of Betty Blair,
who never ever washed her hair ...

A nasty boy named Robert Rung
was always sticking out his tongue ...

Write a cautionary tale of your own, for example about someone who is always picking his nose or who is always boasting, or about someone who does something silly. Write it in rhyming couplets.

Chants

Many chants, like this traditional one, are written in rhyming couplets:

Sam, Sam, the Dirty Old Man

Sam, Sam, the dirty old man,
washed his face in a frying pan.
He combed his hair with a donkey's tail,
and scratched his belly with his big toenail.

Teacher, Teacher

Teacher, teacher, please come quick,
Jennifer Brown's been terribly sick.

Can you complete these "Teacher, teacher" chants?

Teacher, teacher, what should I do? ...

Teacher, teacher, come and have a look ...

Teacher, teacher, look over there . . .

Teacher, teacher, help me please . . .

I Know a Man . . .

I know a man who wears smelly socks.
I know a man who thinks he's a fox.

Can you complete these "I know a man" chants?

I know a man with toes on his head . . .

I know a man whose nose is square . . .

I know a man who lives in a drain . . .

I know a man who's the size of a flea . . .

Homophones

A homophone is one of a group of words that sound the same but have a different meaning or spelling. For example, hare and hair are homophones.

Can you find the homophones in these rhymes?

Bare Bear hasn't any hair.
That's why Bare Bear is bare.

Nobody asked her to dance at all,
   so she had a good bawl at the ball.

"No, I don't know what to do,"
   I said to the man in blue.
"So I'll take my cue from you."

A gnu who was new to the zoo,
  asked another gnu what he should do.
The other gnu said,
  shaking his head,
"If I knew, I'd tell you, I'm new, too!"

Rose grows rows of roses.
Each rose Rose grows, grows in a row.

Now use this dictionary to find homophones for these words:

beach   board   great   need   pale   pane
pear   read   right   road   sell   sew   sore   stair

Which of the above words has more than one other homophone?

Rhyme patterns

Many poems have four-line verses. A four-line verse is called a quatrain.
Quatrains can have a number of different rhyming patterns.

Pattern 1

In this verse the first and second lines rhyme and the third and fourth
lines rhyme.

As I was going out one day,
  my head fell off and rolled away.
But when I saw that it was gone,
  I picked it up and put it on.

Can you complete the second verse of the poem?

And when I got into the ...
  a fellow cried, "Look at your ...!"
I looked at them and sadly ...
  "I've left them both asleep in ...!"

Pattern 2

This poem has verses in which the second line rhymes with the fourth line.

> We are the gremlins.
> We're up to no good.
> We do things we shouldn't,
> not things that we should.
>
> We get up to mischief
> of every sort.
> But we're cunning and clever,
> we never get caught.

Can you complete the next verse of the poem?

> We are the gremlins.
> We disconnect wires ...

Can you add some more verses in the same pattern describing other things that the gremlins do?

Pattern 3

In this verse the first line rhymes with the third line and the second line rhymes with the fourth line.

> When the night is as cold as stone,
> when lightning covers the sky,
> when your blood is chilled to the bone,
> that's the hour when the witches fly.

Can you complete this verse about a mad magician using the same rhyme pattern?

> In his dark cave the mad magician dwells ...

Pattern 4

Sometimes poets write lines in which there is a rhyme within the line. For example:

When Auntie Joan became a phone . . .

This is known as internal rhyme.

In the following verse the second line rhymes with the fourth line and there are internal rhymes in the first and third lines:

Elastic Jones had rubber bones.
He could bounce up and down like a ball.
When he was six, one of his tricks
**   was jumping a ten-foot wall.**

Can you complete this verse using the same rhyme pattern:

Ferdinand Fry boasted, "I can fly!" . . .

Now try to write a poem about a pirate named Peg-Leg Poll in four-line verses, using one of these rhyming patterns.

Index of rhyming sounds

-ab see **crab**
-able see **table**
-ace see **face**
-aced see **paste**
-ack see **back**
-acked see **act**
-act see **act**
-ad see **dad**
-ade see **spade**
-ag see **flag**
-age see **page**
-aid see **spade**
-aight see **gate**
-ail see **tail**
-aim see **name**
-ain see **rain**
-aint see **paint**
-air see **air**
-aire see **air**
-airy see **hairy**
-aist see **paste**
-ait see **gate**
-ake see **lake**
-ale see **tail**
-alk see **talk**
-all see **wall**
-alm see **arm**
-am see **jam**
-ame see **name**
-amp see **stamp**
-an see **van**
-ance see **dance**
-and see **hand**

-ane see **rain**
-ang see **bang**
-ank see **bank**
-anned see **hand**
-ant see **ant**
-ap see **map**
-ape see **grape**
-ar see **car**
-ard see **yard**
-are see **air**
-ark see **dark**
-arm (as in harm) see **arm**
-arm (as in warm) see **storm**
-arred see **yard**
-art see **cart**
-ary see **hairy**
-ase see **face**
-ash see **crash**
-ask see **ask**
-ass see **glass**
-ast see **last**
-aste see **paste**
-at see **hat**
-atch see **catch**
-ate see **gate**
-aul see **wall**
-ave see **cave**
-aw see **score**
-awk see **talk**
-awl see **wall**
-awn see **corn**
-ay see **X ray**

-ayed see **spade**
-ayer see **air**

-ea see **tree**
-each see **beach**
-ead (as in head) see **red**
-ead (as in bead) see **weed**
-eak (as in beak) see **speak**
-eak (as in break) see **cake**
-eal see **wheel**
-eam see **dream**
-ean see **queen**
-eap see **keep**
-ear (as in fear) see **ear**
-ear (as in bear) see **air**
-earn see **urn**
-eas see **freeze**
-ease see **freeze**
-east see **east**
-eat (as in heat) see **meat**
-eat (as in sweat) see **jet**
-eck see **neck**
-ed see **red**
-ede see **weed**
-ee see **tree**
-eech see **beach**
-eed see **weed**

-eek see **speak**
-eel see **wheel**
-eem see **dream**
-een see **queen**
-eep see **keep**
-eer see **ear**
-ees see **freeze**
-eet see **meat**
-eeze see **freeze**
-eg see **leg**
-eigh see **X ray**
-el see **well**
-elf see **elf**
-ell see **well**
-ellow see **yellow**
-elt see **belt**
-en see **hen**
-end see **end**
-ene see **queen**
-ent see **tent**
-ept see **crept**
-er (as in her) see **fur**
-erd see **bird**
-ere (as in here) see **ear**
-ere (as in where) see **air**
-ere (as in were) see **fur**
-ern see **urn**
-erry see **merry**
-ert see **shirt**
-ess see **dress**

143

-essed see **vest**

-est see **vest**

-et see **jet**

-ete see **meat**

-ette see **jet**

-ettle see **nettle**

-ever see **ever**

-ew (as in chew)
see **zoo**

-ew (as in sew)
see **snow**

-ewed see **food**

-ewn (as in sewn)
see **bone**

-ews (as in sews)
see **nose**

-ews (as in news)
see **use**

-ey (as in key)
see **tree**

-ey (as in they)
see **X ray**

-ic see **quick**

-ice (as in ice)
see **ice**

-ice (as in practice)
see **kiss**

-ich see **itch**

-ick see **quick**

-ickle see **tickle**

-icks see **mix**

-ics see **mix**

-id see **lid**

-iddle see **middle**

-ide see **ride**

-idge see **bridge**

-ie see **tie**

-ied see **ride**

-ier see **ear**

-ies see **wise**

-iews (as in views)
see **use**

-ig see **big**

-igh see **tie**

-ighs see **wise**

-ight see **light**

-ign see **nine**

-ike see **bike**

-il see **ill**

-ile see **smile**

-ill see **ill**

-im see **swim**

-ime see **time**

-imp see **imp**

-in see **win**

-ind see **find**

-ine (as in
magazine)
see **queen**

-ine (as in fine)
see **nine**

-ing see **king**

-ink see **ink**

-inner see **dinner**

-int see **print**

-ip see **zip**

-ique see **speak**

-ir see **fur**

-ird see **bird**

-ire see **fire**

-irl see **girl**

-irr see **fur**

-irst see **first**

-irt see **shirt**

-ise (as in rise)
see **wise**

-ise (as in promise)
see **kiss**

-ise (as in paradise)
see **ice**

-ish see **fish**

-iss see **kiss**

-issed see **mist**

-ist see **mist**

-it see **hit**

-itch see **itch**

-ite see **light**

-ive see **five**

-iver see **river**

-ix see **mix**

-ize see **wise**

-o (as in slow)
see **snow**

-oad see **road**

-oak see **oak**

-oal see **hole**

-oap see **rope**

-oar see **score**

-oard see **lord**

-oast see **post**

-oat see **coat**

-ob see **job**

-ock see **knock**

-ocks see **fox**

-ode see **road**

-oe see **snow**

-oes see **nose**

-og see **dog**

-ogue see **dog**

-oil see **oil**

-oke see **oak**

-old see **old**

-ole see **hole**

-oll see **hole**

-ome (as in come)
see **mum**

-on (as in son)
see **sun**

-ond see **pond**

-onder see **under**

-one (as in phone)
see **bone**

-one (as in one)
see **sun**

-oney see **honey**

-ong see **song**

-oo see **zoo**

-ood (as in food)
see **food**

-ood (as in blood)
see **mud**

-ood (as in wood)
see **hood**

-ooed see **food**

-ook see **cook**

-ool see **pool**

-ool (as in wool)
see **pull**

-oom see **room**

-oon see **moon**

-oop see **hoop**

-oot see **boot**

-oor see **score**

-ooze see **use**

-op see **shop**

-ope see **rope**

-or see **score**

-ord see **lord**

-ore see **score**

-ored see **lord**

-ork see **talk**

-orm see **storm**

-orn see **corn**

-ort see **sport**

-os (as in radios) see **nose**

-ose see **nose**

-oss see **boss**

-ost see **post**

-ot see **pot**

-ote see **coat**

-other see **brother**

-ouble see **bubble**

-ough (as in rough) see **puff**

-ough (as in plough) see **cow**

-ought see **sport**

-ould see **hood**

-ounce see **bounce**

-ound see **round**

-oup see **hoop**

-our (as in pour) see **score**

-our (as in hour) see **tower**

-ous see **us**

-ouse see **house**

-out see **out**

-ove see **love**

-ow (as in now) see **cow**

-ow (as in blow) see **snow**

-owed see **road**

-owel see **owl**

-ower see **tower**

-owl see **owl**

-own see **town**

-own (as in phone, groan) see **bone**

-owned (as in crowned) see **round**

-ows see **nose**

-ox see **fox**

-oy see **toy**

-oyal see **oil**

-oze see **nose**

-ub see **grub**

-ubble see **bubble**

-uck see **duck**

-ud see **mud**

-ude see **food**

-ue see **zoo**

-ued see **food**

-ues (as in clues) see **use**

-uff see **puff**

-ug see **jug**

-ul see **pull**

-ule see **pool**

-ull see **pull**

-um see **mum**

-umb see **mum**

-umble see **rumble**

-ume see **room**

-ump see **jump**

-un see **sun**

-unch see **lunch**

-under see **under**

-une see **moon**

-ung see **lung**

-unk see **trunk**

-unny see **honey**

-unt see **hunt**

-up see **up**

-ur see **fur**

-url see **girl**

-urn see **urn**

-urr see **fur**

-urt see **shirt**

-us see **us**

-use see **use**

-ush see **rush**

-uss see **us**

-ust see **dust**

-ut see **hut**

-ute see **boot**

-uy see **tie**

-y see **tie**

-ye see **tie**

-yme see **time**

145

Alphabetical index

cried *92*
cries *123*
crime *111*
crimp *59*
croak *81*
crock *65*
crocodile *100*
crook *21*
crop *99*
croquet *124*
cross *16*
crow *100*
crowed *94*
crown *112*
crowned *96*
crows *80*
crude *40*
crumb *75*
crumble *96*
crunch *70*
crush *97*
crust *30*
cry *110*
cub *47*
cuckoo *128*
cud *75*
cue *128*
cuff *88*
culprit *49*
cup *114*
curious *115*
curl *46*
cursed *39*
cut *55*
cute *15*
cyclist *74*
Czech *78*

D
dab *23*
dad *27*
daffodil *58*
dairy *48*
dale *106*
dam *60*
damp *104*
dance *27*
dandruff *88*
dank *11*
dare *8*
dark *28*
dart *19*
dash *24*
database *34*
date *45*
dawn *22*
day *124*
daydream *29*
dead *91*
deadpan *117*
deadwood *54*
deal *122*
dealt *12*
dear *32*
debate *45*
debt *60*
decade *101*
decay *124*
decayed *101*
deceased *33*
decide *92*
deck *78*
declare *8*
decorate *45*
deed *120*
deep *63*

deer *32*
defeat *72*
defend *33*
defied *92*
define *79*
degree *112*
degrees *42*
delay *124*
delayed *101*
delete *72*
delight *68*
deliver *93*
den *49*
denied *92*
dent *108*
deny *110*
depart *19*
depend *33*
depress *30*
depressed *118*
descend *33*
desert *99*
design *79*
desire *38*
despair *8*
dessert *99*
destroy *112*
detach *19*
detail *106*
detest *118*
devote *20*
devour *111*
dew *128*
dial *100*
dice *56*
did *67*
diddle *73*
die *110*
died *92*

dies *123*
dig *12*
digest *118*
dilute *15*
dim *105*
din *122*
dine *79*
dined *36*
ding *64*
dinner *29*
dinosaur *98*
dip *128*
dirt *99*
disagree *112*
disappear *32*
discard *126*
disco *100*
discuss *115*
disease *42*
disgrace *34*
disgraced *85*
disguise *123*
disgust *30*
dish *39*
dislike *12*
dismiss *65*
dismissed *74*
disobey *124*
display *124*
dispute *15*
distort *103*
distract *8*
distress *30*
distressed *118*
ditch *59*
dive *39*
divide *92*
divine *79*
dock *65*

docks *41*
doe *100*
dog *29*
dolphin *122*
domino *100*
dominoes *80*
done *105*
donkey *112*
donkeys *42*
doom *95*
door *98*
dope *96*
dorm *104*
dot *87*
dote *20*
double *17*
doubt *83*
doubtful *88*
dough *100*
doughnut *55*
dove *70*
down *112*
downed *96*
doze *80*
drab *23*
drag *39*
drain *90*
drank *11*
drape *46*
drawer *98*
drawl *119*
drawn *22*
dread *91*
dreadful *88*
dream *29*
dreg *67*
dress *30*
dressed *118*

drew *128*
dried *92*
dries *123*
driftwood *54*
drill *58*
drink *59*
drip *128*
drive *39*
drone *14*
drool *86*
droop *54*
drop *99*
drought *83*
drown *112*
drowned *96*
drug *61*
drum *75*
drunk *113*
dry *110*
dub *47*
duck *30*
dud *75*
due *128*
duet *60*
dug *61*
dugout *83*
dumb *75*
dump *61*
dune *75*
dung *70*
dungarees *42*
dunk *113*
dust *30*
dwell *120*
dwelt *12*
dye *110*
dyed *92*
dynamite *68*

foul *83*
found *96*
four *98*
fourteen *89*
fowl *83*
fox *41*
fragment *108*
frail *106*
frame *76*
France *27*
frantic *89*
fray *124*
frayed *101*
freak *102*
free *112*
freed *120*
freeze *42*
frequent *108*
fret *60*
fridge *16*
fried *92*
friend *33*
friendship *128*
fries *123*
fright *68*
frill *58*
frog *29*
front *55*
frontier *32*
frown *112*
frowned *96*
froze *80*
fruit *15*
frustrate *45*
fry *110*
fryer *38*
fuel *86*

full *88*
fumble *96*
fume *95*
fun *105*
funny *52*
fur *44*
furious *115*
fuse *116*
fuss *115*

G

gadget *60*
gag *39*
gain *90*
gale *106*
galore *98*
game *76*
gang *10*
gap *71*
gape *46*
gargoyle *81*
gash *24*
gate *45*
gave *20*
gawk *107*
gear *32*
geek *102*
gel *120*
gene *89*
genie *112*
genius *115*
get *60*
ghost *86*
ghoul *86*
gig *12*
gill *58*
gimmick *89*
gimmicks *74*
gird *12*

girl *46*
glad *27*
glance *27*
gland *48*
glare *8*
glass *46*
gleam *29*
glean *89*
glee *112*
glen *49*
glide *92*
glint *87*
glitch *59*
gloat *20*
globule *86*
gloom *95*
glorious *115*
gloss *16*
glove *70*
glow *100*
glowed *94*
glows *80*
glue *128*
glued *40*
glug *61*
glum *75*
glut *55*
gnash *24*
gnat *49*
gnu *129*
go *100*
goal *50*
goat *20*
gob *61*
goblin *122*
goes *80*
gold *82*
good *54*

good-bye *110*
gore *98*
gorgeous *115*
gossip *128*
got *87*
gown *112*
grab *23*
grace *34*
graced *85*
graceful *88*
grade *101*
graffiti *112*
grain *90*
gram *60*
grand *48*
grant *10*
grape *46*
grass *46*
grate *45*
grave *20*
gray *124*
greased *33*
great *45*
greed *120*
Greek *102*
green *89*
greet *72*
gremlin *122*
grew *128*
grid *67*
griddle *73*
grill *58*
grim *105*
grime *111*
grin *122*
grind *36*
grip *128*
grit *49*

groan *14*
grog *29*
groom *95*
grope *96*
ground *96*
group *54*
grow *100*
growl *83*
grown *14*
grows *80*
grub *47*
gruff *88*
grumble *96*
grunt *55*
guarantee *112*
guaranteed *120*
guard *126*
guess *30*
guessed *118*
guest *118*
guide *92*
guitar *18*
gum *75*
gun *105*
guru *129*
gush *97*
gust *30*
gut *55*
guy *110*
gym *105*

H

habit *49*
habitat *49*
hack *13*
had *27*
hag *39*

hail *106*
hair *8*
hairy *48*
hall *119*
ham *60*
hand *48*
handcuff *88*
hang *10*
happiness *30*
hard *126*
hardship *128*
hare *8*
hark *28*
harm *10*
harmful *88*
harpoon *75*
hash *24*
haste *85*
hat *49*
hatch *19*
hate *45*
haul *119*
hawk *107*
hay *124*
haystack *13*
he *112*
head *91*
headache *66*
heal *122*
heap *63*
hear *32*
heard *12*
heart *19*
heat *72*
heed *120*
heel *122*
height *68*
heirloom *95*
hell *120*
hello *100, 127*

know *100*
known *14*
knows *80*

L

lab *23*
label *106*
lace *34*
laced *85*
lack *13*
lacked *8*
lad *27*
lag *39*
lagoon *75*
laid *101*
lair *8*
lake 66
lamb *60*
lame *76*
lamp *104*
lance *27*
land *48*
landmark *28*
landscape *46*
lane *90*
lank *11*
lap *71*
lapel *120*
lard *126*
lark *28*
lash *24*
last 66
latch *19*
late *45*
launderette *60*
lawn *22*
lay *124*

leadership *128*
leak *102*
lean *89*
leap *63*
leaped *26*
learn *115*
least *33*
led *91*
leek *102*
leer *32*
leg 67
lemonade *101*
lend *33*
lent *108*
leotard *126*
less *30*
lest *118*
let *60*
liar *38*
lice *56*
lick *89*
licks *74*
lid 67
lie *110*
lied *92*
lies *123*
light 68
like *12*
likewise *123*
limb *105*
lime *111*
limerick *89*
limousine *89*
limp *59*
line *79*
lined *36*
link *59*

lint *87*
lip *128*
liquid *67*
list *74*
lit *49*
live *39*
liver *93*
load *94*
loan *14*
lob *61*
lock *65*
locks *41*
log *29*
logo *100*
lollipop *99*
lone *14*
loneliness *30*
long *101*
look *21*
lookout *83*
loom *95*
loop *54*
loot *15*
lope *96*
lord 69
lose *116*
loss *16*
lot *87*
louse *54*
love 70
low *100*
loyal *81*
luck *30*
lug *61*
lullabies *123*
lullaby *110*
lumberjack *13*

lump *61*
lunch 70
lung 70
lush *97*

M

macaroni *112*
macaroon *75*
macho *100*
mad *27*
made *101*
magazine *89*
magnet *60*
magnify *110*
maid *101*
mail *106*
maim *76*
main *90*
make *66*
male *106*
mall *119*
man *117*
mane *90*
maniac *13*
manned *48*
map 71
mar *18*
mare *8*
margin *122*
marigold *82*
mark *28*
marmalade *101*
maroon *75*
marred *126*
marvelous *115*

marzipan *117*
mascot *87*
mash *24*
mask *10*
mast *66*
mat *49*
match *19*
matchsticks *74*
mate *45*
matrix *74*
maul *119*
may *124*
me *112*
meadow *100*
meadows *80*
meal *122*
mean *89*
meant *108*
meat 72
meek *102*
meet *72*
megaphone *14*
mellow *127*
melt *12*
men *49*
mend *33*
menu *129*
meow *23*
mere *32*
mermaid *101*
merry 73
mess *30*
messed *118*
met *60*
metal *78*
meteor *98*
mew *128*

mewed *40*
mice *56*
microchip *128*
microscope *96*
microwave *20*
midair *8*
midday *124*
middle 73
midnight *68*
might *68*
mile *100*
mill *58*
millionaire *8*
millipede *120*
mime *111*
mind *36*
mine *79*
mined *36*
mink *59*
mint *87*
minus *115*
minuscule *86*
mischievous *115*
mismatch *19*
misplace *34*
miss *65*
missed *74*
mist 74
mistake *66*
mistletoe *100*
mistook *21*
mite *68*
mix 74

moan *14*
moat *20*
mob *61*
mock *65*
mocks *41*
mode *94*
mold *82*
mole *50*
molecule *86*
Monday *124*
money *52, 112*
monk *113*
monkey *112*
monkeys *42*
monologue *29*
monstrous *115*
moo *128*
mood *40*
mooed *40*
moon *75*
mop *99*
mope *96*
more *98*
morn *22*
mosquito *100*
moss *16*
most *86*
motel *120*
mother *17*
mound *96*
mountaineer *32*
mouse *54*
mow *100*
mowed *94*

mows *80*
muck *30*
mud *75*
muffin *122*
mug *61*
mule *86*
multiply *110*
mum *75*
mumble *96*
munch *70*
mush *97*
mushroom *95*
musketeer *32*
must *30*
mute *15*
my *110*
myself *33*
mysterious *115*
mystify *110*

N
nab *23*
nag *39*
nail *106*
name *76*
nap *71*
near *32*
nearby *110*
neat *72*
neck *78*
need *120*
neigh *124*
neighbor-hood *54*
neighed *101*
nephew *128*
Neptune *75*

nerd *12*
nervous *115*
nest *118*
net *60*
nettle *78*
never *33*
new *128*
news *116*
newt *15*
nice *56*
nicks *74*
night *68*
nightingale *106*
nightmare *8*
nil *58*
nincompoop *54*
nine *79*
nip *128*
no *100*
nomad *27*
none *105*
nook *21*
noon *75*
nor *98*
norm *104*
nose *80*
not *87*
note *20*
noun *112*
now *23*
nude *40*
numb *75*
nun *105*
nursed *39*
nut *55*
nutmeg *67*

O
oak *81*
oar *98*
oat *20*
obey *124*
obeyed *101*
oboe *100*
oboes *80*
obsessed *118*
obtain *90*
obvious *115*
occur *44*
octopus *115*
ode *94*
offend *33*
office *65*
oil *81*
okay *124*
old *82*
omelette *60*
omit *49*
one *105*
ooze *116*
operate *45*
oppress *30*
or *98*
orangutan *117*
orbit *49*
ordeal *122*
ore *98*
organize *123*
origin *122*
ornament *108*
ostrich *59*
other *17*
otter *44*
ounce *16*
our *111*

out *83*
outdoor *98*
outfit *49*
outlaw *98*
outrage *84*
outright *68*
overhang *10*
overlap *71*
ow! *23*
owe *100*
owed *94*
owl *83*
own *14*
ox *41*
ozone *14*

P
pace *34*
paced *85*
pack *13*
packed *8*
pact *8*
pad *27*
page *84*
paid *101*
pail *106*
pain *90*
paint *85*
pair *8*
pale *106*
palm *10*
pan *117*
pancake *66*
pane *90*
pang *10*
pant *10*
pantomime *111*
parachute *15*

parade *101*
paradise *56*
parakeet *72*
parallel *120*
park *28*
part *19*
pass *46*
passed *66*
passport *103*
past *66*
paste *85*
pat *49*
patch *19*
pâté *124*
patio *100*
patrolled *82*
pave *20*
pawn *22*
pay *124*
pea *112*
peach *11*
peak *102*
peal *122*
pear *8*
pearl *46*
peas *42*
peat *72*
peck *78*
pedigree *112*
peek *102*
peel *122*
peep *63*
peer *32*
peg *67*
pelt *12*
pen *49*
penguin *122*
perform *104*
perfume *95*
permit *49*

persuade *101*

Peru *129*

pest *118*

pet *60*

petal *78*

petrifies *123*

pew *128*

phew *128*

phone *14*

photo *100*

piano *100*

pick *89*

pickle *109*

picks *74*

pickup *114*

pie *110*

pier *32*

pies *123*

pig *12*

piggyback *13*

pigsty *110*

pike *12*

pile *100*

pill *58*

pillow *100*

pin *122*

pine *79*

ping *64*

pink *59*

pioneer *32*

pit *49*

pit-a-pat *49*

pitch *59*

pixie *112*

place *34*

placed *85*

plain *90*

plan *117*

plane *90*

plank *11*

planned *48*

plaque *13*

plate *45*

platoon *75*

played *101*

playful *88*

playwright *68*

plea *112*

plead *120*

please *42*

plight *68*

plop *99*

plot *87*

plow *23*

ploy *112*

pluck *30*

plug *61*

plum *75*

plumb *75*

plume *95*

plump *61*

plunder *114*

plus *115*

plush *97*

pocket *60*

poke *81*

pole *50*

polite *68*

poll *50*

polled *82*

pollute *15*

pond 85

pool 86

pop *99*

pope *96*

porridge *16*

port *103*

pose *80*

possess *30*

possessed *118*

post 86

postcard *126*

postpone *14*

pot 87

potato *100*

potatoes *80*

pounce *16*

pound *96*

pour *98*

poured *69*

pout *83*

power *111*

powwow *23*

pox *41*

practice *65*

prance *27*

prank *11*

pray *124*

prayed *101*

prayer *8*

preach *11*

precious *115*

precise *56*

prefer *44*

preferred *12*

prepare *8*

present *108*

press *30*

pressed *118*

pretend *33*

prevent *108*

prey *124*

preyed *101*

price *56*

prick *89*

pricks *74*

pride *92*

prim *105*

prime *111*

primp *59*

princess *30*

print 87

prize *123*

profile *100*

program *60*

progress *30*

progressed *118*

promise *65*

promote *20*

prone *14*

pronounce *16*

prop *99*

propel *120*

propose *80*

prose *80*

protest *118*

provide *92*

provoke *81*

prowl *83*

prune *75*

pry *110*

pub *47*

puff 88

puffin *122*

pull 88

pump *61*

pumpkin *122*

pun *105*

punch *70*

punish *39*

punk *113*

punt *55*

pup *114*

puppet *60*

purr *44*

purred *12*

pursued *40*

pus *115*

putt *55*

pyramid *67*

Q

quack *13*

quacked *8*

quail *106*

quake *66*

queen 89

quest *118*

quick 89

quill *58*

quit *49*

quite *68*

quiver *93*

quote *20*

R

rabbit *49*

raccoon *75*

race *34*

raced *85*

rack *13*

radio *100*

radios *80*

radius *115*

rag *39*

rage *84*

raid *101*

rail *106*

railway *124*

rain 90

rainbow *100*

rake *66*

ram *60*

ramp *104*

rampage *84*

ran *117*

rang *10*

rant *10*

rap *71*

rapid *67*

rare *8*

rash *24*

rat *49*

rat-a-tat *49*

rate *45*

rave *20*

ray *124*

reach *11*

react *8*

real *122*

realize *123*

reap *63*

rear *32*

rebel *120*

reboot *15*

recent *108*

recipe *112*

recite *68*

recline *79*

recognize *123*

recoil *81*

recommend *33*

record *69*

red 91

reed *120*

reek 102
reel 122
referee 112
refereed 120
referees 42
refrain 90
refugee 112
refuse 116
regard 126
regret 60
rehearsed 39
reign 90
rein 90
released 33
rely 110
remain 90
remark 28
remind 36
remote 20
rendezvous 129
renowned 96
rent 108
repair 8
repeat 72
replace 34
replaced 85
replies 123
reply 110
report 103
reptile 100
request 118
rescued 40
resent 108
resign 79
resist 74
resort 103
respond 85
rest 118
retreat 72

return 115
reveal 122
revere 32
revise 123
revive 39
revue 128
reward 69
rewind 36
rhyme 111
rice 56
rich 59
ricochet 124
rid 67
riddle 73
ride 92
ridge 16
ridicule 86
rig 12
right 68
rigid 67
rim 105
ring 64
rink 59
rip 128
rise 123
river 93
road 94
roar 98
roared 69
roast 86
rob 61
robin 122
robot 87
rock 65
rocket 60
rocks 41
rode 94
rodeo 100
role 50
roll 50

rolled 82
rook 21
room 95
root 15
rope 96
rose 80
rot 87
rough 88
round 96
rout 83
routine 89
row 100
rowed 94
rows 80
royal 81
rub 47
rubbish 39
rubble 17
rude 40
rug 61
ruin 122
rule 86
rum 75
rumble 96
rump 61
run 105
rung 70
runny 52
runt 55
rush 97
rust 30
rut 55

S
sack 13
sacked 8
sacrifice 56
sad 27
sag 39
said 91

sail 106
saint 85
sake 66
saloon 75
salute 15
same 76
sand 48
sane 90
sang 10
sank 11
sap 71
sardine 89
sash 24
sat 49
satin 122
satisfy 110
save 20
say 124
scab 23
scaffold 82
scale 106
scam 60
scan 117
scanned 48
scant 10
scar 18
scare 8
scarecrow 100
scarred 126
scary 48
scene 89
scent 108
schedule 86
scheme 29
school 86
scold 82
scoop 54
scoot 15
scope 96

score 98
scoreboard 69
scored 69
scorn 22
Scot 87
scour 111
scout 83
scowl 83
scram 60
scrap 71
scrape 46
scratch 19
scrawl 119
scream 29
screech 11
screen 89
screw 128
screwed 40
screws 116
scrimp 59
scroll 50
scrub 47
scruff 88
scrunch 70
scuff 88
sea 112
seal 122
seam 29
seas 42
seat 72
secret 60
see 112
seed 120
seek 102
seem 29
seen 89
seep 63
sees 42
seize 42

self 33
selfish 39
sell 120
send 33
sent 108
separate 45
sequin 122
serene 89
serious 115
service 65
set 60
settle 78
sever 33
severe 32
sew 100
sewn 14
sews 80
shack 13
shade 101
shadow 100
shadows 80
shake 66
shallow 100
sham 60
shame 76
shampoo 128
shampooed 40
shape 46
share 8
shark 28
shave 20
shawl 119
she 112
shear 32
shed 91
sheen 89
sheep 63
sheer 32

sheet 72
shelf 33
shell 120
shin 122
shine 79
ship 128
shirt 99
shiver 93
shock 65
shocks 41
shoe 129
shoelace 34
shoo 128
shooed 40
shook 21
shoot 15
shoot-out 83
shop 99
shore 98
shorn 22
short 103
shot 87
should 54
shout 83
shove 70
show 100
showed 94
shower 111
shown 14
shows 80
shrank 11
shred 91
shrew 128
shriek 102
shrill 58
shrimp 59
shrine 79
shrink 59
shrub 47

shrug 61
shrunk 113
shun 105
shunt 55
shush 97
shut 55
shy 110
sick 89
sickle 109
side 92
sigh 110
sighed 92
sighs 123
sight 68
sign 79
signed 36
signpost 86
sill 58
sin 122
sincere 32
sing 64
sink 59
sinner 29
sip 128
sir 44
sit 49
site 68
six 74
size 123
skate 45
skateboard 69
ski 112
skid 67
skies 123
skill 58
skim 105
skimp 59
skin 122
skip 128

skirt 99
skis 42
skunk 113
sky 110
slab 23
slack 13
slam 60
slang 10
slant 10
slap 71
slapdash 24
slash 24
slate 45
slave 20
sled 91
sleek 102
sleep 63
sleet 72
sleigh 124
slept 26
slew 128
slice 56
slick 89
slid 67
slide 92
slight 68
slim 105
slime 111
sling 64
slink 59
slip 128
slipper 44
sliver 93
slog 29
sloop 54
slop 99
slope 96
slot 87
slow 100
slowed 94

slows 80
slug 61
slum 75
slump 61
slung 70
slunk 113
slur 44
slush 97
sly 110
smack 13
smacked 8
small 119
smart 19
smash 24
smear 32
smell 120
smile 100
smoke 81
smother 17
smug 61
snack 13
snacked 8
snag 39
snail 106
snake 66
snap 71
snare 8
snatch 19
sneak 102
sneer 32
sneeze 42
snip 128
snitch 59
snob 61
snoop 54
snooze 116
snore 98
snored 69
snort 103
snot 87

snout 83
snow 100
snowed 94
snowflake 66
snows 80
snub 47
snuff 88
snug 61
so 100
soak 81
soap 96
soar 98
soared 69
sob 61
sock 65
socks 41
software 8
soil 81
sold 82
sole 50
solitaire 8
solitude 40
solo 100
some 75
someone 105
son 105
song 101
soon 75
sore 98
sorrow 100
sort 103
soul 50
sound 96
soup 54
sour 111
souvenir 32
sown 14
sows 80
space 34
spaced 85

spade 101
Spain 90
span 117
spank 11
spanned 48
spar 18
spare 8
spark 28
sparred 126
spat 49
speak 102
spear 32
speck 78
sped 91
speech 11
speed 120
spell 120
spend 33
spent 108
spice 56
spied 92
spies 123
spike 12
spill 58
spin 122
spine 79
spinner 29
spire 38
spit 49
spite 68
splash 24
splat 49
spleen 89
splice 56
splint 87
split 49
spoil 81
spoke 81
spool 86
spoon 75